MIX
Papier aus verantwortungsvollen Quellen
Paper from responsible sources
FSC® C105338

Maximilian Margolin

Managerial Overconfidence

Different Thinking through Different Education

Anchor Academic
Publishing

Margolin, Maximilian: Managerial Overconfidence: Different Thinking through Different Education. Hamburg, Anchor Academic Publishing 2013

Buch-ISBN: 978-3-95489-128-3
PDF-eBook-ISBN: 978-3-95489-628-8
Druck/Herstellung: Anchor Academic Publishing, Hamburg, 2013

Bibliografische Information der Deutschen Nationalbibliothek:
Die Deutsche Nationalbibliothek verzeichnet diese Publikation in der Deutschen Nationalbibliografie; detaillierte bibliografische Daten sind im Internet über http://dnb.d-nb.de abrufbar.

Bibliographical Information of the German National Library:
The German National Library lists this publication in the German National Bibliography. Detailed bibliographic data can be found at: http://dnb.d-nb.de

Hermannstal 119k, 22119 Hamburg
http://www.diplomica-verlag.de, Hamburg 2013
Printed in Germany

Table of contents

List of Figures

List of Tables

List of Abbreviations

CHF	–	Swiss Franc
CEO	–	Chief Executive Officer
CFO	–	Chief Financial Officer
C. A.	–	California
C. T.	–	Connecticut
DAX	–	Deutscher Aktienindex
eds.	–	editors
e.g.	–	exempli gratia
et al.	–	et alii
fMRI	–	functional magnetic resonance imaging
ICFA	–	Institute of Chartered Financial Analysts of India
JoF	–	Journal of Finance
M&A	–	mergers and acquisitions
M. A.	–	Massachusetts
N.J.	–	New Jersey
N.Y.	–	New York
NPV	–	Net Present Value
OLS	–	Ordinary Least Squares
PhD	–	Doctor of Philosophy
pp.	–	pages
Univ.	–	University
US	–	United States
USA	–	United States of America
USD	–	United States Dollar

1 Introduction

Many models in business and economics are based on the assumption that agents are "rational". Barberis and Thaler (2003) propose two characteristics of what a "rational" agent is. The first one is that the agents update their beliefs according to Bayes' law when they receive new information. The other characteristic is that the agent's choices are consistent with Savage's notion of Subjective Expected Utility. Countless experiments and observations in the field show, however, that these seemingly obvious characteristics are far from natural for humans.

Daniel Kahneman received the Nobel Memorial Prize in Economic Sciences in 2002 "for having integrated insights from psychological research into economic science, especially concerning human judgment and decision-making under uncertainty" (Nobel Foundation, 2008) He and many other prominent researchers have studied what assumptions of standard economic and financial models tend to be violated by actual human behavior, how those models could be adapted and, most importantly, why humans behave irrationally in the first place.

Looking for explanations of individual economic behavior in psychology is nothing new and can be traced back as far as to Adam Smith's *The Theory of Moral Sentiments* (1759). Only during the last 50 years, however, have researchers like Kahneman, Tversky or Thaler begun to differentiate between individual cognitive biases and to study their impact on human behavior. Psychology has thereby gained a much higher relative value in economics and business and the idea of bound rationality has become a grave challenge for existing economic models.

1.1 Purpose of this Study

De Bondt and Thaler (1995) claim that "perhaps the most robust finding in the psychology of judgment is that people are overconfident". In literature overconfidence has been blamed for economic bubbles and crises (Scheinkman and Xiong, 2003) as well as for international conflicts and wars (Johnson, 2004). Consequently, much research was conducted on the bias termed "overconfidence", its roots and effects. These studies showed that overconfidence plays an important role in various fields like economics, finance, management or entrepreneurship. Understandably factors influencing an individual's level of overconfidence have been of particular interest for researchers. In this context research has identified many factors, some more and some less amenable to influence. The question is therefore whether the factors found so far are conclusive or whether other factors of influence also exist.

The purpose of this study is to investigate this very question and to argue in favor of an individual's major field of study as a factor of influence not studied yet. I propose that the field in which an individual has been educated in the sense of whether it is rather quantitatively or rather qualitatively oriented influences a person's mode of thought and there over influences her proneness to overconfidence. While education has already been shown to impact one's level of overconfidence previous research focused on the length and profoundness of education. The study at hand, however, examines the connection between overconfidence and the field in which a person has been educated. The issues covered are therefore how education and mind set are related, why a differentiation between "quantitative" and "qualitative" education makes sense in this context, and how different mind-sets influence an individual's proneness to overconfidence.

1.2 Course of Investigation

This study is divided into two main parts: a literature review of the concept of overconfidence and an argumentative part where I propose quantitative education as a factor influencing an individual's level of overconfidence that has not been investigated so far. First I shall describe the concept of overconfidence by presenting essential definitions and introducing managerial overconfidence as a special form of overconfidence. In addition to this I will present research regarding sources of overconfidence as well as consequences of overconfident behavior in the areas of finance, management, entrepreneurship, and economics.

After the theoretical foundation has been laid, I will present the results of a previous experiment as well as results from an empirical data set of German top managers. In both cases differences in individual levels of overconfidence can be observed, that cannot be explained by factors traditionally assumed to influence overconfidence. Since the only systematic connectedness seems to be that individuals from the fields of mathematics, natural sciences, and engineering exhibit lower levels of overconfidence I propose that these differences could stem from dissimilarly strong quantitatively oriented education of the subjects.

As a possible explanation for why such a relationship might exist, I suggest that focus of education may have an influence on individual levels of overconfidence through distinct ways of reasoning that are acquired and practiced during higher education. In order to corroborate this hypothesis I present the concept of *dual processes of reasoning* according to which humans use two distinct cognitive systems. I support my initial hypothesis with findings form psychological research showing that people make distinct use of these reasoning systems depending on how they have been educated. I further argue that the use of one of these systems fosters overconfidence while the other one inhibits it. Therefore, an individual's disposition towards overconfidence could be influenced by the predominant use of one of these systems. Proceeding from this I will give an outline of an experimental design in which my hypothesis could be tested. After a brief summary of my arguments I end with concluding remarks.

2 Concept of Overconfidence

The term “overconfidence” might seem difficult to define. In economic literature it is often used as an umbrella term for a variety of effects and phenomena. At its hearts seems to be the notion that people tend to be optimistic in situations of uncertainty. The concept as a whole, however, remains vague. In the following chapter I will discuss the theoretical framework of the concept of overconfidence and clarify the different aspects that are subsumed under this term. Alongside with the presentation of conceptual work on overconfidence and its appearance I shall describe managerial overconfidence as a special form of overconfidence. Additionally I will present criticism that has been expressed regarding the bias itself as well as current methods used to demonstrate it.

2.1 Theoretical Concept

Baberis and Thaler (2002) differentiate between two manifestations of overconfidence: too narrow confidence intervals and bad assessment of probabilities. This differentiation is based on results from two different experiments. The first one is a confidence interval estimation game in which subjects are asked to report an interval for which they are X% sure that a certain variable, such as the number of murders in the USA in a certain year, lies in this interval. Alpert and Raiffa (1982) found that in such a setting the true number fell in their subjects’ 98% confidence intervals only 60% of the time. The second type of experiment uses a design in which subjects have to assess the probability of a certain random event. Fischhoff, Slovic and Lichtenstein (1977) found that events which subjects deemed certain occurred only with an 80% probability while events which the subjects considered impossible still occurred with approximately 20 % probability.

These two aspects are revisited by Ben-David, Graham and Harvey (2010). In an empirical analysis of stock market forecasts made by U.S. financial executives, the authors find that managers use too narrow confidence intervals while underestimating the element of chance. When asked to estimate future stock market returns, only 39% of the true returns fell into the executives’ forecasted 80% confidence intervals. Calling this finding a “miscalibration”, the authors equated the combination of the two aspects addressed by Baberis and Thaler with overconfidence.

The concept of miscalibration is also taken up by Englmaier (2007) in his review of overconfidence literature. While Ben-David, Graham and Harvey use the term as synonym with overconfidence, Englmaier refers to it as just one possible manifestation of overconfidence. Englmaier proposes that, apart from miscalibration, there are three other main outward forms of overconfidence, namely self-serving bias, illusion of control, and overoptimism.

Self-serving bias refers to people's tendency to attribute success to their own abilities while blaming failure on external circumstances (Miller and Ross, 1975). The authors argue that people who expect a certain outcome tend to overestimate their influence on the outcome once it occurs. Fischhoff (1982) takes up this notion of people's self-serving tendency and suggests that, after the occurrence of an uncertain outcome individuals forget their original forecasts and adjust their memory to fit the actual outcome. Furthermore, according to Fischhoff, people retrospectively exaggerate how certain they were about the outcome in the beginning.

Illusion of control, the second manifestation of overconfidence according to Englmaier, is the notion that individuals are often mistaken about the extent to which they can control future events while underestimating chance (Langer, 1975). In Langer's original series of experiments, subjects perceived their likelihood of winning in a lottery to be higher when they could pick the numbers themselves rather than being given numbers by an external source. Further experimental evidence is presented by Allan and Jenkins (1980) from experiments in which subjects could press or not press a button resulting in a light flash or not. The authors conducted the experiment with two groups of subjects. One group could technically determine by a certain probability the reaction of the light by their decision to press or not press the button, while for the other group the light's reaction was entirely random. Even though subjects in the second group had no influence on the light they still reported to have the impression that they were the ones controlling the light.

Overoptimism, which is the fourth outward appearance of overconfidence according to Englmaier, refers to people's tendency to be overly optimistic about the outcome of their actions. This often goes along with underestimation of the likelihood of unfavorable outcomes. One of the first studies to approach overoptimism is Marks (1951). In a simple card drawing game with nine to twelve-year old children, Marks found that subjects' reported expectations of the outcomes of the (random) card drawings were influenced by the desirability of the outcome. Irwin (1953) confirmed this finding for adults by showing that even grown-up subjects believed the likelihood of a random card drawing to be higher when a certain card was favorable and lower when it was unfavorable. Weinstein (1980) also showed that people believe that good things will happen to them more often than to others.

If self-serving bias is formulated as people's tendency to overestimate their abilities, then miscalibration could be one possible manifestation of such an overestimation. The combination of these two forms of overconfidence makes Englmaier's four forms of overconfidence identical to the three positive illusions leading to an unrealistically positive attitude towards oneself described by Taylor and Brown (1988) as well as Kruger et al. (2009).

2.2 Managerial Overconfidence

The term managerial overconfidence is generally used without explicit definition in research when referring to overconfident behavior of individuals in managing positions and its consequences. Nicolosi (2006) explicitly questions whether corporate executives can be expected to fall prey to the same cognitive bias as experimental subjects and individual investors. Using financial data from US companies, the author investigates this question and finds that even if individual executives exhibit behavior that is associated with overconfidence, companies and markets account for this and the resulting effects are insignificant.

Contrary to Nicolosi, most studies on the matter of overconfidence do not make a distinction between "ordinary" experimental subjects and corporate executives. Moreover, there are numerous studies showing that managers do exhibit overconfidence (e.g. Malmendier and Tate, 2005a; Malmendier and Tate, 2005b; Ben-David et al., 2006). Consequently, the question rises as to why overconfidence of corporate executives has been granted so much attention in financial literature.

Statistical regressions with data from corporate policies and individual CEO characteristic coefficients have shown that individual characteristics of top-level executives are significantly related to corporate decisions (Bertrand and Shoar, 2003). Barber and Odean (2001) sum up that overconfidence is greatest for tasks that are difficult, when making forecasts where the outcome has a low predictability, and during undertakings that lack fast and clear feedback. All these characteristics are typically met in managerial decision environments. This means that corporate managers are, on the one hand, the most prone to overconfidence and, on the other hand, their decisions can harm the most if biased. This "double danger" makes managerial overconfidence and its consequences particularly interesting for research.

2.3 Criticism

Countless studies show experimental findings, which researchers have interpreted as evidence for the cognitive bias of overconfidence. Overconfidence seems to have been an accepted fact, and research focused on the reasons for and the consequences of this bias when some researchers started calling it into question in the 1990s. Instead of the concept of overconfidence as a cognitive bias, researchers proposed rational explanations for the behavior formerly interpreted as overconfidence.

In economic literature, one common way of demonstrating overconfidence is asking subjects to answer general knowledge questions and then ask them to indicate their level of certainty of their answer's correctness. Erev et al. (1994) criticize this method and argue that the discrepancy between accuracy and level of confidence when answering a question may also result from a regression effect. They describe the probability of a correct answer to a test question as a function of knowledge and the element of chance, since a question, particularly a multiple-choice question, can also be answered correctly by guesswork. When looking at accuracy as a function of the level of certainty because of the element of chance the authors show the existence of a regression effect. The predicted accuracy lies closer to the average which means that accuracy is relatively lower for high levels of certainty and relatively higher for low levels of certainty. This argumentation is consistent with the hard-easy effect.[1] Erev and colleges' point is revisited by Budescu et al. (1997) as well as Klayman et al. (1999). Both studies estimate the unsystematic error in their experiments in order to distinguish between unsystematic error and systematic bias. The authors find that systematic overconfidence exists, but, due to unsystematic errors, it is smaller than previously assumed.

More criticism is raised by Gigerenzer et al. (1991) and Juslin (1994) who challenge the fairness of the questions used in overconfidence-experiments. These authors claim that when choosing two-choice questions (e.g. Which city has more inhabitants? Dortmund or Dresden?), experimenters tend to take misleading ones which are answered wrong rather than right if the subject does not know the answer with certainty. According to Gigerenzer et al. the subject constructs a probabilistic mental model when being confronted with such a question. If they do not know the correct answer with certainty people consider general cues like "has an airport", "famous sights" or "large companies' headquarters" in order to assess the cities' sizes. The criticism is that researchers often choose pairs for which the subject would answer

[1] See chapter 3.2.5 for an explanation of the hard-easy effect.

wrongly using such cues and therefore mislead subjects. In the aforementioned example a subject would probably think Dresden is larger than Dortmund because it is much more famous in terms of architecture and culture and has an international airport. Dortmund would, however, be the correct answer as it has around 581,000 inhabitants while Dresden has only 530,000. In an experiment Gigerenzer and his colleges showed that overconfidence disappears if test-questions are chosen randomly and representatively. This argument was revisited by Brenner et al. (1996) and again by Klayman et al. (1999). Neither study could replicate the results of Gigerenzer et al.

A very basic point is furthermore made by Svenson (1981), who addresses one of the classical ways to demonstrate overconfidence, namely to ask subjects if they are better than the average in a certain area (e.g. car driving). In most studies that use this method, significantly more than 50% of the subjects place themselves as better than average which is logically impossible and commonly interpreted as overconfidence.[2] Svenson points out that different people may have different definitions of being skillful in the areas studied (e.g. car driving skills could be measured by the number of traffic warrants received or the number of accidents had or prudence perceived by other drivers and so on) and, therefore, theoretically all the subjects assessing themselves as above average could be in fact merely mean above average as according to their personal definition.

Benoît and Dubra (2011) take up this method of demonstrating overconfidence and challenge the notion that people's tendency to regard themselves as better than average automatically indicates overconfidence, as it is mostly found in economic literature. The authors argue that (wrongly) placing oneself above the average based on performance in a certain task can be perfectly Bayes-rational if one does not have any contradicting information available. Benoît and Dubra use the example of car drivers of low, middle, and high skill. Given that the probability of a low-skilled driver to have an accident is the highest and the probability of a high-skilled driver is the lowest a driver who has never before had an accident would rationally place herself as high-skilled. This, however, might be wrong and the real reason she has never had an accident was pure luck. Nevertheless the authors do not challenge the notion of overconfidence itself but rather question the validity of certain experimental evidence.

The criticism presented in this chapter is appropriate and benefits research on overconfidence. Challenging certain methods of demonstrating overconfidence allows for a more valid analysis and interpretation of experimental and empirical data. It stresses the importance of

[2] See chapter 4.1 for a discussion of the better-than-average effect.

clear differentiation between rational, albeit seemingly odd behavior and the real irrational bias of overconfidence. In the following chapter I will examine the concept of overconfidence more closely by presenting research on the sources of this bias as well as factors influencing its appearance.

3 Sources of Overconfidence

Some authors propose explanations for such "irrational" behavior as overconfidence deliberately excluding systematic biases from human judgment. For example Stanovic and West (2000) see performance errors, human computational limitations, wrong norms being applied by experimenters and differences in the comprehension of a task by subjects as the four main reasons. In this study, however, I follow the more prominent school of thought which regards overconfidence as a cognitive bias keeping while in mind the critical points discussed in the previous chapter. In this chapter, I will first explore the reasons for overconfident behavior examined so far and in a second step review studies on factors influencing the extent to which people show overconfidence.

3.1 Principal Sources

One explanation for the origins of overconfidence is presented by Griffin and Tversky (1992). According to them, the reason why people are overconfident is their biased mode of processing information. The authors divide information into two elements, strength and weight. By strength they refer to the potential importance of information, such as the magnitude of the consequences of an event. By weight they refer to the credibility or reliability of the information. Griffin and Tversky claim that overconfidence is the consequence of a focus on strength of information while its weight is being adjusted. If, on the contrary, a person emphasizes weight while subordinating the strength of information, the result is underconfidence.

A slightly different approach is taken by Koriat et al. (1980) and Klayman and Ha (1989). They also blame people's assessment of information in a decision-making process for overconfidence but suggest that the main reason is people's selective perception of evidence. In their eyes people tend to quickly draw conclusions and then focus on evidence supporting it while irrationally neglecting any information to the contrary. Similarly McKenzie (1997) argues that overconfidence occurs because people focus on evidence for and against a quickly drawn first conclusion while ignoring any alternative conclusions with information supporting them.

Both approaches are based on the idea that once a decision is made people tend to hold on to it and are unlikely to change it even if there is evidence against their decision. This argumentation is supported by cognitive dissonance theory. Knox and Inkster (1968) conducted an experiment in which they asked people before and right after they placed their bets in a horse race about how certain they were that their horse would win. The results showed that right after the decision was made the better's confidence level rose, which the authors interpreted as post-decisional dissonance reduction. Similarly, Frenkel and Doob (1976) found that voters' confidence that their preferred candidate would win rose right after the casting of their vote. In both studies subjects reduced emotional discomfort caused by imagined failure through mentally adjusting the probability of a loss. Both studies dealt with decisions that are ultimate and cannot be changed. Koriat et al. (1980), Klayman and Ha (1989) as well as McKenzie (1997) confirmed these findings for interlocutory decisions in a judgmental process and showed that post-decisional dissonance reduction could still well occur on this micro-decision level.

Another psychological factor that evokes overconfidence is an individual's self-image (Blanton et al., 2001). According to Blanton et al. every individual has a desire to see herself as competent and knowledgeable. This self-image hinders self-doubt and leads to an irrational confidence in one's own decisions. Fiske and Taylor (1991) add that confident behavior is often perceived as an indication of competence. Therefore, even if an individual has an accurate self-assessment, she might want to cast herself in a better light, which leads to underassessment of risks and increased confidence.

Russo and Schoemaker (1992) present three more generalized reasons for overconfidence: cognitive bias, physiological causes and motivational factors. Furthermore, they subdivide the element of cognitive bias into availability bias, anchoring bias, confirmation bias, and hindsight.

Availability bias refers to a concept introduced by Tversky and Kahneman (1973). They claim that people assess the likelihood of an event depending on how easily they can remember similar outcomes. An example for this judgmental heuristic would be that many people highly overestimate the number of shark attacks because the picture of a shark attacking a human comes to mind very easily due to horror movies and excessive news coverage of singular events. Judgments based on this heuristic are often misleading and can promote overconfidence as probabilities are assessed wrongly.

The second heuristic that misleads people and thus promotes overconfidence is anchoring bias. This concept introduced by Tversky and Kahneman (1974) refers to the tendency of people to rely irrationally heavily on single pieces of information during a decision-making process. Russo and Schoemaker presented questions to subjects, in which a number (e.g. the length of the river Nile) had to be guessed. One group had to make a best guess first and then come up with a 90% confidence interval around this number. This resulted in the subjects taking their first guess as an anchor point and then choosing too narrow confidence intervals. The other group of subjects was asked to immediately provide a confidence range without making a first guess. As a consequence they choose more accurate confidence intervals and thus showing less overconfidence.

The concept of confirmation bias, which Russo and Schoemaker see as a third bias leading to overconfidence, refers to people's tendency to seek confirming evidence once a first prediction has been made while ignoring any disconfirming evidence. Russo and Schoemaker integrate the ideas of Koriat et al. (1980) and Klayman and Ha (1989) described above. As in previous studies, Russo and Schoemaker raise awareness for the consequences of wrong assessment of arguments used in a decision-making process that result from confirmation bias.

The fourth and last cognitive bias Russo and Schoemaker propose to be responsible for overconfidence is hindsight, which is the illusion of predictability of an outcome in retrospect. First investigated by Fischoff and Beyth (1975) hindsight bias is accountable for people's impression that many uncertain events are much more predictable than they really are. Russo and Schoemaker consider this false assessment of chance an important reason for wrong assessment of own forecasting accuracy and thus an unduly confident behavior.

In addition to the mental causes presented above Russo and Schoemaker point at biochemical processes as a possible physiological explanation for overconfidence. The authors claim that hormones, such as adrenalin and endorphins, produced in the human body as a response to strong emotional reactions, lead to exaggerated self-confidence. Russo and Schoemaker draw a parallel to the effects of alcohol: just like alcohol inhibits a person's response time and thus one should not drive under the influence of alcohol, strong emotions facilitate overconfidence and therefore one should not make decisions while in an emotional agitation.

As a third factor, the authors propose the vital motivational effect of confident behavior. Russo and Schoemaker point at the psychological finding that optimism has motivational value. According to them, an individual's performance in a certain task highly depends upon her motivation for success. A confident, and thus easily overconfident, attitude is indispensable for motivation. The authors quote German poet Johann Wolfgang von Goethe, who wrote, "for a man to achieve all that is demanded of him he must regard himself as greater than he is." Furthermore, the authors argue that people often equate confidence with competence. Hence, people cannot afford to appear unconfident given they do not want to be considered incompetent.

3.2 Influencing Factors

The concepts presented above provide possible reasons for overconfidence. However, the occurrence of overconfident behavior also depends upon several factors impacting the probability that an individual will fall prey to overconfidence as well as the extent to which she will differ from a rational view. In the following I will more closely examine such factors and current literature on how fostering or inhibiting those factors seem to be.

3.2.1 Age

In a study of university students who had to predict their own performance prior to a test as well as their expected performance after the test Grimes (2002) found that although the students were relatively homogenous with respect to age (average age of 20.5 years; standard deviation of less than 2.2 years), age was a statistically highly significant factor for the level of overconfidence. While younger students showed a high level of overconfidence, older students were much more accurate in their self- assessment. Similar results are presented by Bertrand and Schoar (2003). Studying data of large U.S. firms and their top executives the authors find that older managers tend to be more conservative while younger managers take more risks and exhibit greater confidence.

However, when studying age as a factor influencing overconfidence, it is difficult to separate age from experience. Malmendier and Nagel (2010) studied individuals who experienced economic depressions and booms in their life to see whether macroeconomic experience influences risk taking behavior. They found that people who had experienced a great depression were less willing to take financial risks, while individuals who mainly experienced high stock returns were less averse to risk. If the degree of risk aversion which is often linked to the extent of overconfidence is influenced by events like the great depression in the 1930s or the "Wirtschaftswunder" (economic boom) in Germany in the 1950s, this is a serious factor of distortion when correlation between age and overconfidence is studied.

3.2.2 Education

When assessing education as a factor influencing the level of overconfidence, two contradictory effects might come to mind: On one hand the better a person is educated the more competent she becomes and the higher her accuracy can be expected to be. On the other hand, education, especially for young people just out of school, could give an individual an illusion of safety and lead to overestimation of actual abilities. While both possibilities are realistic, most psychological literature supports the second one.

One example of education hampering overconfidence is discussed by Lundeberg et al. (1994). In an experimental bidding game with male and female undergraduate and graduate students, the authors find that undergraduate students, especially male ones, exhibit more overconfidence than graduate students in the study.

Contrary to that, Graham et al. (2009) find that their constructed measure of investors' self-perceived competence and thus their overconfidence is highly positively correlated with the investors' undergraduate and graduate education. This is supported by Mayhew and Simpson (2002), who argue that, in the context of driving safety, special drivers' education in emergency maneuvers and collision avoidance techniques fosters the drivers' overconfidence. Thus, paradoxically, special training increases the risk of an accident rather than reducing it.

The hypothesis that education fosters overconfidence rather than decreasing it is also supported by empirical evidence from professionals in the field of finance. In a study of U.S. CFOs' forecasts about stock market returns as well as the corresponding confidence intervals given by the CFOs, Ben-David et al. (2006) find that the better the CFOs were educated, the more they exhibited overconfidence as measured by miscalibration of their forecasts.

3.2.3 Gender

Stereotypically men are often considered to show more overconfidence than women. There is a lot of empirical and experimental evidence suggesting that this is indeed the case. According to Nowell and Alston (2007), male students exhibit greater overconfidence than their female fellow students when asked to predict their grade at completion of a university course. Similarly, Soll and Klayman (2004) show in a classical year guessing experiment with confidence intervals, that male subjects overestimate their accuracy more than female subjects.

Similar evidence also exists for business-related decisions. In a Gallup poll for PaineWebber with approximately 15,000 between 1998 and 2000 individual investors were asked to predict the total market return as well as the return of their own portfolio for the next twelve months. According to Barber and Odean (2001) as well as Graham et al. (2005), this data shows that both, men and women, on average predicted to outperform the market, but men did so significantly more.[3] Combining this data with the idea that overconfidence leads to excessive trading and ultimately to underperformance, Barber and Odean (2001) analyzed trading data of male and female individual investors.[4] Their results show that male investors trade more than their female counterparts and perform less well, which again confirms the assumption that men show more overconfidence than women when it comes to financial decisions.

However, gender differences in overconfidence seem to depend on the task studied. Lundeberg et al. (1994) argue that gender differences can be found mainly in areas perceived to be masculine domains. In accordance with this theory, Lichtenstein and Fischhoff (1981) did not find any gender differences for the levels of overconfidence for general knowledge questions. Dunning et al. (2003) found that female subjects who had to evaluate their performance on typically male-oriented tasks rated themselves worse than even those male subjects who exhibited underconfidence.

3.2.4 Cultural Background

The consensus among researchers seems to be that cultural background does influence the level of overconfidence although it is disputed how exactly it does so and what the reasons for this influence could be. In a groundbreaking study Wright et al. (1978) asked British and Hong-Kong subjects to answer multiple-choice questions while stating how certain they were about their answers. The researchers obtained results that served as the basis for much further research. Both groups of subjects were overconfident about the correctness of their answers, but the Asian subjects were significantly more overconfident than their Western counterparts.

Yates et al. (1996) as well as Yates et al. (1997) offer two different explanations for why Asians might be more overconfident than individuals from Western cultures. In their first paper the authors offer the differences in education systems as one explanation. According to them in Western cultures students are generally encouraged to think critically whereas in

[3] Men predicted an outperformance of the market by 2.8 percentage points while women predicted an outperformance by 2.2 percentage points. (t = 3.3).
[4] See chapter 4.2.1 for further discussion.

Asian cultures tradition plays a large role and viewpoints of others as well as oneself are challenged much less. This hypothesis is supported by evidence form an overconfidence comparison study between Chinese students from Fujian and Chinese students from Singapore. Li et al. (2006) conducted an experiment to investigate whether Chinese students would also exhibit more overconfidence in comparison to students from Singapore, even though the Singaporean students were descendants from Fujian-Chinese and therefore shared a common culture and cultural heritage. The authors could thereby more or less eliminate other cultural factors and isolate the effects of different educational systems. The results confirmed the authors' hypothesis that Singaporean students educated based on Western standards were less overconfident than the Chinese students.

In Yates et al. (1997) the difference in expression of convincement is added as another possible explanation for different levels of overconfidence. Since in Asian cultures the saving of face is crucial, individuals from Asian cultures often express certainty about something they do not know because admitting to not knowing something would result in a loss of face.

A different approach is taken by Weber and Hsee (1998). These researchers studied transaction prices of financial options and showed through experiments that Chinese subjects underestimated risks in this field more strongly than American subjects. The authors offer the explanation that because of Chinese collectivism and their culture of solidarity, risks are perceived as lower than they would be in American culture where risks are generally borne individually. This hypothesis is tested in Hsee and Weber (1999). The authors studied risk-aversion of Chinese and American subjects in several different areas. The results showed that a significant difference in risk perception can be found only when it comes to financial risks, but not in academic or medical situations. With financial losses, Chinese society might step in to help the individual. In academia and medicine, however, risks are normally borne individually in both cultures. This confirms the authors' hypothesis that the nature of risk bearing is the reason for the observed cultural differences.

3.2.5 Task Familiarity and Performance

It is obvious that competence and experience in a certain task increase accuracy. The question, however, of how they affect confidence has been studied with very different results. Langer (1975) studied the impact of familiarity with a setting on overconfidence. He gave some subjects lottery tickets which were familiar to them, while another subject group received unfamiliar ones. The result was that even perceived familiarity with a setting (winning still depended on pure chance as all tickets had the same likelihood of winning) increased the illusion of control over the outcome and thus overconfidence of subjects. These findings suggest that experience and familiarity with a task generally increase overconfidence as individuals feel saver and perhaps more daring in familiar environments.

The notion that task familiarity fosters overconfidence while unknown and difficult tasks decrease it is mentioned by Lichtenstein, Fischhoff and Phillips (1980) as the hard-easy-effect, meaning that with hard tasks, typically, underconfident behavior can be observed and for easy tasks mainly overconfidence occurs.

This is also supported by Hoelzl and Rustichini (2005), who had their subjects take a vocabulary test with easy and difficult words. Afterwards, subjects could vote whether the pay-off for the experiment should depend upon the relative performance of each subject (the best 50% would receive a payment of about 10 USD) or based on a lottery in which a randomly determined 50% of the subjects would receive the payoff of 10 USD. The vast majority of subjects solving the easy test voted for the payoff to depend upon relative performance, while most subjects solving the difficult test preferred the lottery. The authors interpret this behavior as the subjects confusing "being good" with "being better". Subjects solving the easy test anticipated a good absolute performance and transferred their good feeling to relative performance. Thus familiarity with the vocabulary tested fostered overconfidence while dealing with unfamiliar words and thus an unfamiliar task had the opposite effect.

Contrary to these results, Oskamp (1965) finds in a study of clinical judgment that while both, professional psychologists and psychology students, exhibit overconfidence in their judgment professionals with years of experience do so less than inexperienced students. Ben-David et al. (2006) find in their CFO stock market prediction study that, on top of education as a factor that increases miscalibration, overconfidence is negatively correlated with professional experience.

A possible explanation for these contradictory findings is given by Gervais and Odean (2001). They propose that the effect of experience and familiarity on overconfidence cannot be determined generally but depends upon the degree of experience. Early in an individual's career she has acquired little experience while having the illusion of competence and experience. At this stage, overconfidence is increased by experience. Later, in a professional career, the person might have gained more insight and learned to account for overconfidence, so that experience then decreases overconfidence.

The studies presented above generally show that experience does have an effect upon overconfidence, while questioning whether this effect is positive or negative. Nevertheless some renowned studies found that experience has no effect on overconfidence at all. Both, Lichtenstein and Fischhoff (1977) and Allen and Evans (2005) could not show a statistically significant correlation between experience and overconfidence using data from an experimental bidding game.

3.2.6 Feedback

One reason why feedback may reduce overconfidence is that with increasing quantity and quality of available information, accuracy of assessment also increases. Park and Santos-Pinto (2010) compared overconfidence of poker and chess players, whom they asked to predict their relative performance before a tournament. Although both groups were found to overestimate their performance, on average the poker players' predictions were close to random guesses while the chess players were much more accurate and less overconfident. The authors explain these results with the different roles that luck and skills play in the two games. In poker, luck is accountable to a much higher degree for a player's performance. A player, therefore, has limited information for predictions. In chess, skill is far more important, and, based on previous performance, a player learns receives more reliable information about her skills. Thanks to the additional information, chess players' predictions become more accurate and allow for less overestimation. This follows the "Pollyanna Principle" formulated in Matlin and Strong (1978). The principle states that the less reliable the information used in a decision-making process is, the more favorably it is interpreted. Thus, ambiguous information leads to more overconfidence than clear and detailed information.

The reduction of overconfidence through feedback can also be explained by two other factors. Bornstein and Zickafoose (1999) state that overconfidence of subjects decreases when subjects learn about the existence of overconfidence. Subjects do not even need to get feedback about their own level of overconfidence, but they rather take into consideration that they might act overconfidently after their attention has been drawn to this bias. This means that it is not just specific feedback, but also the general awareness of overconfidence that counterbalances it.

Moreover, Allen and Evans (2005) conclude that feedback generally reduces the level of confidence regardless of whether an individual exhibits overconfidence, underconfidence or sophistication. In an experimental financial market the authors identified that 40% of subjects were overconfident. Feedback about individual levels of overconfidence reduced individual confidence not only for subjects who had been overconfident beforehand, but throughout the participants. This general reduction of individual levels of confidence naturally also led to less overconfidence.

3.2.7 Importance of a Topic

Blanton et al. studied an individual's self-image as a source of overconfidence and discovered another factor influencing overconfidence: the importance of a topic. If the perceived importance of a topic to an individual is high, a wrong decision or answer would cause greater harm to the individual's self-perception as a competent and knowledgeable person. (Blanton et al., 2001) The harmfulness of potential failure increases confidence in decisions and therefore raises the level of overconfidence. Frank (1935) was one of the first researchers to show a connection between importance of a task and overestimation of abilities. He used simple motor-skill tasks, like printing words against time, to study the factors influencing a person's motivation in a task.

This is consistent with Koehler et al. (2002), who compared and analyzed data of American and Dutch lawyers' assessment of their chances of winning a case with the real outcome of the case. Koehler et al. discovered that American lawyers, who work on a contingency fee basis, are more overconfident than their Dutch colleagues, who charge fixed hourly fees regardless of the outcome of the case. Since the payment of American lawyers depends upon success at court, the outcome of the case matters more to the American lawyers than to their Dutch counterparts, which explains the difference in the level of overconfidence.

3.2.8 Mental Condition

Although it may seem obvious that mental illness can impact overconfidence, even what is considered „good mental health" is accompanied by a moderate level of overconfidence. Taylor and Brown (1988) suggest that overconfidence is essential for mental health and that healthy people are always overconfident. Taylor (1989) goes a step further by stating that an accurate self-assessment, at least in Western cultures, goes along with minor depression.

Apart from mental illness, personality traits of a person influence overconfidence. (Schaefer et al., 2003). Out of the "Big Five" factors of personality, which are openness to experience, conscientiousness, extraversion, agreeableness, and neuroticism, extraversion significantly predicts overconfidence (Schaefer et al., 2003).[5] Even though openness to experience was correlated with confidence, it also predicted accuracy rather than overconfidence as such.

3.2.9 Situational Factors

The level of overconfidence is also influenced by situational circumstance. According to Russo and Schomaker (1992), confidence is often equated with and perceived as competence. Especially in situations where persuading or impressing someone is important an individual might want to seem particularly competent and therefore act in a confident or *over*confident manner.

Another situation-dependent aspect is the complexity of a decision. Ronis and Yates (1987) argue that whenever people have to make a decision, they reduce the complexity of a setting. For this purpose they discard information that is not intuitively crucial. This reduction of complexity can lead to underestimation of risks and consequently to overconfidence. The more complex a situation is, the more information has to be discarded and the more overconfidently the person may act.

[5] See Tupes and Cristal (1961) for the original framework of the Big Five character traits and Goldberg (1990) for further development.

4 Implications of Overconfidence

After having discussed the theoretical framework of overconfidence in the preceding chapters, I will now present literature dealing with the impacts of overconfidence on individual behavior in a business context. Based on economics and business related literature, the most important areas of impact of overconfidence are finance, entrepreneurship, management, and economics. A mutual basis for impacts of overconfidence in these areas is the better-than-average effect. Thus, I shall first introduce this notion before proceeding with impacts of overconfidence observed in the respective areas.

4.1 Better-Than-Average Effect

In numerous studies, subjects have been asked to assess their performance on a certain task or to assess certain fixed personal qualities relative to those of their peers. Regardless of whether subjects had to assess academic performance, professional skills, or items like the quality of their relationships, basically all studies have one finding in common: the majority of subjects constantly rate themselves as above average. In a survey, 87% of MBA students at Stanford University assessed their academic performance as above average (Zuckerman and Jost, 2001). When asked to assess their driving skills, 93% of surveyed Americans as well as 69% of Swedish students rated themselves above average (Svenson, 1981). Despite being told that, on average, every second marriage ends in divorce, the median answer of young couples applying for a marriage license was 0% when asked how likely they considered a divorce at some point of their marriage would be (Baker and Emery, 1993).

While one might argue that young couples about to get married are not the most rational group of subjects when it comes to self-assessment, the results of the studies mentioned before are striking. This tendency to rate oneself as above average has been termed the better-than-average effect and is considered one of the most robust self enhancement phenomena (Alicke and Govorun, 2005; Taylor and Brown, 1988; Sedikides and Gregg, 2003).

The biased assessment of abilities that derives from overconfidence is a major problem for financial investors, entrepreneurs, and managers whose behavior can have vast financial consequences for themselves and others. Because of its generality in application the better-than-average effect provides a common basis for various individual implications of overconfidence which I will discuss in the following sections.

4.2 Implications for Finance

Research on consequences of overconfident behavior for finance can be split into research on consequences for individual investors on the one hand and consequences for companies on the other hand. Therefore, I will split the relevant into literature on security trading (main area of interest for individual investors) as well as such on M&A and corporate investments (main areas of interest for companies in the context of overconfidence).

4.2.1 Implications for Security Trading

Overconfidence has a major effect on security trading by increasing trading activity. Varian (1989) suggests that heterogeneous beliefs about the value of an asset are essential for significant trading. Based on this, Benos (1998) and Odean (1998) formulate the hypothesis that overconfident traders overestimate private information and accordingly the expected profits from a trade. As a consequence, they engage in costly trading activities, which rational investors would not do. This "overtrading" lowers the expected utility of overconfident investors as compared to rational ones. Analyzing data from 10,000 customer trading accounts from 1987 to 1993, Odean (1999) empirically confirms that overconfidence leads to excessive trading and lowers investors' returns. Investors "overtrade" to such an extent that, in Odean's sample, the stocks bought on average underperformed the stocks sold.

DeLong et al. (1990) point out that with overconfident investors, whom they call "noise traders", prices of assets are much more volatile and can diverge significantly from the fundamental value of those assets. This creates a higher risk for sophisticated investors. The authors mention that overconfident investors underestimate the risk of assets and heavily invest in risky assets, thereby raising their prices and unbalancing their price/return proportions. This idea is taken up by Daniel et al. (2001) who also consider overconfident investors responsible for market overreactions. The authors suggest a model, in which expected security returns are not only determined by an asset's intrinsic risk, but also by the risk of investor misvaluation.

Scheinkman and Xiong (2003) go as far as blaming overconfident investors for speculative bubbles. They consider heterogeneous beliefs of overconfident and sophisticated investors about assets' values the reason for investors' willingness to pay more for assets than what their actual value would be. Like in the "greater fool theory" investors value the option to later-on sell an asset to another investor at a higher price. Hence they are willing to buy assets at prices exceeding their own valuation which can lead to speculative bubbles.

Although the idea that overconfident investors underperform sophisticated investors seems to be prevalent in finance literature, Kyle and Wang (1997) argue that in a theoretical model with risk-neutral investors, overconfidence can strictly dominate rationality. They regard an agent's trading strategy as a trading-quantity choice in a standard Cournot duopoly. According to the authors, overconfidence serves as a commitment device, giving the overconfident trader a reputation for trading aggressively and making the rational investor trade less. Consequently, overconfident investors facing rational opponents can make more profit than rational ones.

4.2.2 Implications for M&A

During mergers and acquisitions the bidding firm often places its bid higher than the market's valuation of the target firm. In addition to explanations from classical corporate finance, such as potential synergies or tax saving opportunities justifying a premium, Roll (1986) brought forth managerial hubris as another potential explanation. Empirical evidence for the hypothesis that overconfidence leads to exaggerated transaction bids is, for example, presented by Hietala, et al. (2003). Analyzing the acquisition of Paramount by Viacom in 1994, the authors find that Viacom had overpaid its acquisition by approximately $2 billion out of the total price of $9.2 billion. They blame hubris, as suggested by Roll, as the main reason for this overpayment.

Building on those findings, Billet and Qian (2008) explore acquisitions of overconfident managers over the time of their careers. The authors present the hypothesis that overconfident managers fall prey to self-attribution of successful past acquisitions, and, therefore, even successful acquirers perform worse the more deals they operate. Using a sample of acquisitions by U.S. companies between 1985 and 2002, Billet and Qian focused on frequent acquirers, that is managers who acquired more than two companies over a period of 5 years, and confirmed their hypothesis.

In addition to the problems of overpayment for a target company and the progressively deteriorating performance of managers over the course of their career Malmendier and Tate (2008) find that overconfident CEOs are more likely to make acquisitions in general and low-quality deals in particular when sufficient internal funding is available to them. According to the authors, the market anticipates such value-destroying behavior and reacts significantly more negatively to a merger announcement when the bidding company's CEO is portrayed as overconfident by the media.

4.2.3 Implications for Corporate Investment

While other topics in finance have been approached with behavioral additions to traditional models for decades, corporate investment is a rather young field for behavioral finance. Heaton (2002) was among the first to propose managerial overconfidence as a reason for corporate misinvestment. According to the author, two factors are critical when it comes to overconfident managers: on the one hand, they overestimate the returns of their investment projects, and, on the other hand, they believe their company is undervalued by the market. The author argues that an overly optimistic manager who overestimates the returns of a risky project will overinvest and, thereby, destroy shareholder value. Furthermore, since overconfident managers overestimate their company's value, they regard external financing, especially equity, as too costly. Therefore, they might underinvest, turning down projects with a positive NPV if external funding is necessary to carry out those projects.

This idea is taken up by Malmendier and Tate (2005b), who follow Heaton's line of argument that an overconfident manager will strongly prefer internal over external financing. The authors conclude that, as long as managers use internal funding they are not disciplined by the market for misinvestments and will consequently overinvest as long as internal funding is available.

A different facet is studied by Barros and da Silveira (2008). They state that overconfident managers will prefer a higher leverage for financing their firm. In traditional finance, a company's optimal level of leverage is a trade-off between the tax advantages of debt financing and the rising bankruptcy costs of high leverage. Barros and da Silveira argue that an overconfident manager will systematically underestimate bankruptcy risks and costs and will, therefore, adjust a too high leverage. Using data from publicly listed Brazilian companies between 1998 and 2003, the authors empirically confirm their hypothesis by showing that their constructed measure of overconfidence is strongly positively correlated with the corresponding company's leverage ratio.

4.3 Implications for Entrepreneurship

As in the example of young couples who, contrary to what statistics suggest, uniformly believe that their marriage will not end in divorce, entrepreneurs are unlikely to seriously entertain the thought that their business might fail. No rational person would undertake a costly and time-consuming venture without the firm belief that their company will flourish. Cooper et al. (1988) found in a sample of 2,994 entrepreneurs that 81% of their subjects estimated the success chances of their business to be at least 70%. 33% of the subjects even believed that their venture would be successful with 100% probability. Nevertheless, the ten-year survival rate for single businesses opened in 1992 was around 29%, so not only did many businesses fail but, in the long run, seven out of ten businesses failed (Shane, 2008).

Koellinger et al. (2007) propose that overconfidence is a central reason for such high failure rates. The authors studied data from 29 countries collected in 2001 by Global Entrepreneurship Monitor, an academic project studying entrepreneurial behavior. They discovered, unsurprisingly, that the strongest entrepreneurial propensity is people's belief in themselves, their skills and their ability to start a business. More surprisingly, the authors also found out that the level of self-reported confidence is significantly negatively correlated with a company's survival chances. The authors go even further by suggesting that certain countries exhibit higher start-up activities because their inhabitants are generally more (over-) confident than people living in counties with lower levels of entrepreneurial activities.

De Meza and Sothey (1996) add that the standard learning model for entrepreneurs, in which they enter the market uncertain of their abilities and then learn from experience, while the less able drop, out might not hold. The authors argue that, in reality, new entering entrepreneurs are dominated by those who are disproportionally overconfident. As a consequence, banks offering startup financing account for the overconfidence of entrepreneurs who seek credit. Consequently, even if a rational or pessimistic individual considered self-employment she would regard the bank's financing offer as unfair and pass on becoming an entrepreneur.

Bernardo and Welch (2001) highlight the importance of entrepreneurs for the evolutionary process of a group. The authors designed their study around the notion that distribution of private information is essential for evolutionary progress. Since members of a group tend to herd in their behavior they do not reveal private information and the group' information aggregation stays poor. Entrepreneurs, however, do not follow the group, but their own, private information. By acting this way, they reveal their private information to the group and improve its information aggregation. Even when they make irrationally overconfident choices which are detrimental to themselves, entrepreneurs act altruistically, by sacrificing themselves for the group. Overconfident entrepreneurial behavior is most beneficial if the group is large enough to benefit from positive information externality the most, if the individuals' information is low-precision, and if overconfidence is moderate rather than extreme (Bernardo and Welch, 2001).

4.4 Implications for Management

Russo and Schoemaker (1992) suggest that overconfidence of managers is neither generally good nor generally bad, but that it depends on the position of a manager. When it comes to strategic decision making, overconfidence is harmful because managers underestimate risks and overestimate future returns. Managers can, however, benefit from overconfidence when their behavior becomes more motivating and inspiring through their confidence and perceived competence. Englmaier (2006) supports this view and stresses optimism, high involvement, and increased effort which employees put into their work if they are overconfident. Thus, overconfident managers are worse decision makers but more inspiring leaders than their rational counterparts and therefore better suited as mid-level managers who implement decisions rather than top-level managers who make them. This is adverse, since according to Han et al. (2009) as well as Goel and Thakor (2008), overconfident employees are promoted more often and, especially when competing for executive positions, overconfident candidates are at an advantage. This means that companies could very well benefit from overconfident managers but they tend to put them in the wrong position, which results in loss rather than profit.

Another important aspect of overconfidence in the context of management is a low willingness to learn. Miller (1999) argues that overconfident individuals have fixed reference points and are less willing than rational individuals to deviate from these points. This leads to a low openness to new methods and hinders progress and learning.

4.5 Implications for Economics

One topic in economics where overconfidence plays a role is market entries. Camerer and Lovallo (1999) created as a variation of Kahneman (1988) a setting in which subjects had to decide whether or not to enter a market. If they decided to stay out of the market, they received a small, fixed payoff. If, however, the subject decided to enter the market, their payoff depended on a ranking within the market and only a certain number of the highest ranked participants received a payoff. To study the effect of overconfidence, the researchers used two different ways of ranking the subjects: one group of subjects were told that they would be ranked according to their result in a preceding logic-puzzle test, while the other half was told that ranking is done randomly. The authors found, that participants chose to enter the market more excessively when their payoff depended on their relative skills rather than being a random assignment. Overconfident agents overestimated their own skills and ignored the fact that other agents might also regard themselves as skilled. Thus, they entered the market and made it more competitive. According to the authors, overconfidence generally results in excessive and highly inefficient market entries.

Overconfidence becomes also interesting for economists in contract design in principal-agent settings. Malmendier and Tate (2008) studied the influence of overconfidence on manager's acquisition actions and found, among other aspects, that overconfident managers who overpay for target companies honestly believe that they are maximizing their shareholders' value. Therefore, such managers inadvertently destroy value, even though their contracts might feature incentives to make sure they protect shareholders' interests. The authors propose that overconfident managers' sub-optimal investment decisions can be better controlled by financial constraints and close control than by standard incentive contracts.

Almazan et al. (2007) highlight two ways in which overconfidence impacts welfare: investment in human capital and clustering of companies. The authors studied location choice of companies in knowledge-based industries and argue that efficient firms tend to form regional clusters because they value the opportunity to hire employees trained by competitors. Thereby, they increase the competition over human capital in the region, which decreases incentives for a firm to invest in employee training because employees can sell their labor at a high market price. Consequently, rational agents underinvest in human capital in clusters. Overconfident agents, however, overvalue the efficiency of their companies and seek clusters even if direct competition were to ultimately ruin their own company. Furthermore, they overvalue their ability to hold on to well-trained employees and invest more in human capital than a rational agent would. Overconfidence thus increases welfare by, on the one hand fostering direct competition and driving inefficient firms out of the market and, on the other hand, offsetting rational agents' underinvestment in human capital.

Santos-Pinto (2011) considers the interaction of overconfidence and investment in training as a reason for the pay gap between male and female workers. According to Santos-Pinto, overconfident individuals will underestimate their cost of acquiring a high education and will, therefore, invest more in education than rational or underconfident individuals. Since men tend to be more prone to overconfidence than women, they will, accordingly, also invest more in education. Assuming that men and women are, by nature, equally productive and that education increases productivity, this means that, due to their overconfidence, men's productivity and thus their salaries increase more than those of their female co-workers.

5 Motivation for my Research

As stated in the introduction, the purpose of this study is to argue in favor of the major field of study as a factor influencing an individual's level of overconfidence. In the following chapter, I will present empirical as well as experimental evidence suggesting that there are systematic differences in proneness to overconfidence between individuals from quantitative and rather qualitative fields of study. This evidence will be the motivation for my further investigations.

5.1 Empirical Evidence

I studied the overconfidence of the CEOs of the largest German companies. German top managers are well suited for studying overconfidence and its links to education, because the members of German executive boards mainly come from fairly heterogeneous groups: lawyers, economists, engineers, and natural scientists. Traditionally, in Germany lawyers have always been a well-represented group among top executives. However, in the last decade, the number of lawyers declined in favor of engineers and natural scientists. Still, there are currently enough CEOs with each respective educational background to allow for a systematic analysis of the groups.

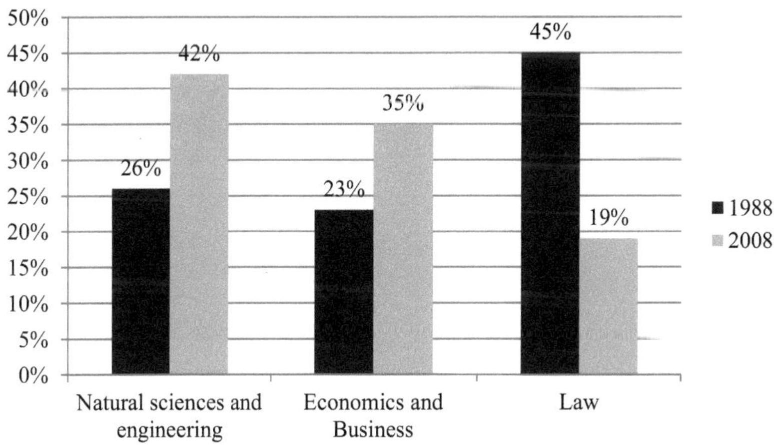

Figure 1: Academic Education of German DAX-Company CEOs

Source: Odgers Berndtson (2009)

5.1.1 Data

To construct a data set, I looked at all managers, who during the last 20 years served as CEO of one of the publicly quoted companies, which were included in the German DAX in the last 20 years. A period of 20 years is long enough to provide a sufficiently large number of executives while still ensuring comparability. This provided me with a subject pool of 129 managers from 47 different companies.

Previous research offers many possible methods for the assessment of overconfidence. Since conducting an experiment with CEOs as subjects seems impractical for the purpose of this paper, I shall use openly observable public behavior of the executives to measure their overconfidence. One easy way of assessing managerial behavior is by evaluating press reports. Malmendier and Tate (2008) find that press portrayal is a reliable measure of an executive's level of overconfidence. Building on this, I shall use the relative number of instances in which a CEO is described as confident or overconfident as a proxy of overconfidence. Because of the lack of an adequate translation of the word "overconfident" in German I will use the keywords "selbstbewusst" (self-confident), "selbstsicher" (self-assured) and "überzeugt" (sure of oneself). I searched for these keywords in major German financial newspapers and business magazines, which were provided by the database Factiva and recorded for each manager how often his name appears in articles and how often he is described as "sebstbewusst", "selbstsicher" or "überzeugt".[6] For this search, I used articles published over the last 20 years, that is publications between 1st January, 1992 and 31st December, 2011. In order to ensure validity of results, only managers who appear in a minimum of 300 articles are included in the analysis. This eliminates 52 of the aforementioned executives.

The resulting data set includes 77 managers, out of which 74 possess a university degree and three completed an apprenticeship. Of those holding degrees, 33 are engineers or natural scientists, 28 have a degree in business or economics, 18 studied law, and two majored in humanities. With one exception, all university-educated managers hold a Master-equivalent degree and 47 hold an additional PhD. The average age at which the managers have been appointed CEO is 51.8 years. Nearly two thirds were appointed between the ages of 45 and

[6] For a complete list of the magazines and newspapers used see appendix 1.

55, the youngest being 37 and the oldest 60 at the time of appointment. The dataset includes only male CEOs.[7]

In the following analysis, the managers are grouped according to their field of study with respect to quantitative and qualitative education. Natural sciences and engineering can be considered the most quantitative, while law and the humanities are rather qualitative subjects based on the role mathematics play in the respective fields. Business and economics lie between these two distinct groups, depending on the chosen concentration and will therefore be regarded as intermediate. An apprenticeship as a form of professional education can be regarded as less quantitative and is therefore grouped together with law and the humanities. Five CEOs in the data set studied more than one of the differentiated subjects. Those managers are assigned to a group based on which of their degrees is more quantitative.

5.1.2 Results

The results of mean scores across fields of education are presented below.[8]

Table 1: Average Overconfidence of German CEOs According to Press Portrayal

Educational background	**N**	**Average Score**	**Standard Deviation**
Law and Humanities	18	6.05%	1.23% points
Business and Economics	26	5.62%	1.83% points
Engineering and Natural Sciences	33	5.09%	1.63% points
Total	77	5.49%	1.65% points

Source: own research

The results show that a week, but systematic difference in levels of overconfidence between managers from different educational backgrounds can be observed. On average, managers

[7] The original pool of 129 managers included only one female CEO (Manuela Better of Hypo Real Estate). However, her name appeared in only 74 articles and she is therefore excluded from the analysis. It is worth noting that she is the only female DAX-company CEO over the past 20 years and was only appointed CEO in 2010 when Hypo Real Estate was already bankrupt and had been excluded from the DAX for two years.

[8] For a complete table with results of all 77 CEOs see appendix 2.

with a rather qualitative educational background are described as confident and self-assured 20% more often than their counterparts with a quantitative background. Consistent with the initial placement of executives with business or economics background as in-between the strictly quantitative or qualitative groups, their overconfidence score as approximated by press portrayal lies in between the two other groups.

To test whether the observed difference is statistically significant, I used the Kruskal-Wallis-test. Similar to the Mann-Whitney-U-test this non-parametric test uses rank sums of groups of values in order to determine whether those groups belong to the same population. The statistic H, which is χ^2-distributed, is defined by the following formula:

$$H = \frac{12}{n(n+1)} \sum_{h} \frac{S_h^2}{n_h} - 3(n+1)$$

The degree of freedom associated with this variance estimate is calculated as df = k-1, with k being the number of groups.

In my case, H is approximately 236.52 and df is 2. The null hypothesis being that the three groups are from the same population is rejected for $\alpha = 0.01$ if H exceeds the critical value of 10.6. Consequently the null hypothesis is rejected because the difference between the two groups is significant at any reasonable significance level.

One could argue that the meaningfulness of this non-parametrical test is lower than that of the more commonly used Student's t-test. For this reason I, also run Welch's t test on my data. This adaptation of the original Student's t-test is used whenever it cannot necessarily be assumed that the populations from which the samples are taken have equal variances. The statistic t is defined by the following formula:

$$t = \frac{\overline{X}_1 - \overline{X}_2}{\sqrt{\frac{s_1^2}{N_1} + \frac{s_2^2}{N_2}}}$$

The degree of freedom υ associated with this variance estimate has to be approximated with the Welch-Satterthwaite equation:

$$\nu = \frac{\left(\frac{s_1^2}{N_1} + \frac{s_2^2}{N_2}\right)^2}{\frac{s_1^4}{N_1^2 \cdot \nu_1} + \frac{s_2^4}{N_2^2 \cdot \nu_2}} = \frac{\left(\frac{s_1^2}{N_1} + \frac{s_2^2}{N_2}\right)^2}{\frac{s_1^4}{N_1^2 \cdot (N_1-1)} + \frac{s_2^4}{N_2^2 \cdot (N_2-1)}}.$$

Since I wanted to test the difference in confidence between CEOs from quantitative and qualitative educational backgrounds, the null hypothesis is H_0: $\mu_{qual} - \mu_{quant} = 0$, while the alternative hypothesis is H_1: $\mu_{qual} - \mu_{quant} > 0$.

Using the formula above, the results are $t = 2.36$ and $\upsilon = 43.80$. The critical value of t at $\alpha = 0.05$ is 2.02, and, therefore, the null-hypothesis can be rejected at this significance level. The difference in confidence levels between managers with quantitative and the ones with qualitative educational backgrounds is significant up to a level of $\alpha = 0.011$.

A regression controlling for factors known to influence overconfidence might be interesting for further analysis. From the factors that have been discussed to influence overconfidence in chapter 3.2, only a few can be reasonably controlled for. Since all managers in the data set are male and of very similar cultural backgrounds, it makes sense to control for education, age, and experience.[9] To control for age differences, the variable *AGE* takes on the age at which the respective manager was appointed CEO. *YEARS* controls for differences in experience by taking on the number of years the respective manager has stayed in office. To control for different educational backgrounds, I used the dummy variables *EDU* and *PHD* where *EDU* takes the value of 1 if a manager has a quantitative education as defined in 5.1.1 and 0 if not. *PHD* takes the value of 1 if the respective CEO has a PhD degree and 0 if not. The dependent variable is *CONFI* which takes the level of overconfidence of the respective CEO as approximated via press portrayal. Thus, to see whether quantitatively educated CEOs in the sample are less overconfident controlled for other differences, the following equation is estimated by OLS:

$$CONFI = \beta_0 + \beta_1\, EDU + \beta_2\, PHD + \beta_3\, AGE + \beta_4\, YEARS + \epsilon_i.$$

The results of this regression are shown below.

[9] With exception of Hakan Samuelsson (MAN, Sweden) and Harry Roels (RWE, Netherlands) all managers in the sample studied come from Germany, Austria or Switzerland.

Table 2: Output from the Regression

Source	SS	df	MS		
Model	.003790838	4	.000947709	Number of obs =	77
Residual	.016789823	72	.000233192	F(4, 72) =	4.06
				Prob > F =	0.0050
				R-squared =	0.1842
				Adj R-squared =	0.1389
Total	.020580661	76	.000270798	Root MSE =	.01527

confi	Coef.	Std. Err.	t	P>|t|	[95% Conf.	Interval]
edu	-.0062203	.003586	-1.73	0.087	-.0133689	.0009282
phd	.0005907	.003584	0.16	0.870	-.006554	.0077353
age	.0007953	.0003508	2.27	0.026	.000096	.0014946
years	.0013114	.0004472	2.93	0.005	.0004199	.0022029
_cons	.006664	.0191853	0.35	0.729	-.0315812	.0449093

The results show that, consistent with previous research, overconfidence is significantly positively correlated with age and experience. As for education, both variables *EDU* and *PHD* are not significant, but *EDU* is close to being so. While a PhD degree, and thus a more lengthy education, seems to have no influence on the level of overconfidence, managers from quantitative fields are less overconfident than others at a significance level of at least 91.3%.

One reason why a PhD degree might not have the expected effect on overconfidence is that in German-speaking countries, a PhD is a degree by research, which can be added after regular studies at the master's level have been completed. Studies indicating that a lengthier education correlates with overconfidence are mostly from North America, where a PhD is to a larger extent a taught degree, often following undergraduate studies. Therefore, a PhD in North America significantly extends a student's education while in German-speaking countries it should be less count against a person's education but rather professional research career.

More important for the purpose of this paper is that the variable *EDU* shows the expected negative correlation with confidence, which, however, is not significant. This could have several reasons: first of all, it should be investigated whether the linear regression model applied here is suitable. A Skewness/Kurtosis test for Normality reveals that the hypothesis that residuals are normally distributed cannot be rejected. Furthermore, a Breusch-Pagan/ Cook-Weinberg test for heteroscedasticity test does not provide any indication that the assumption of homoscedasticity might be violated. Also, calculating the correlations of independent variables shows that the model is not biased by multicollinearity.

Table 3: Correlations of Independent Variables

	confi	edu	phd	age	years
confi	1.0000				
edu	-0.2158	1.0000			
phd	-0.0221	0.0461	1.0000		
age	0.1754	0.1100	-0.0300	1.0000	
years	0.3147	-0.1725	-0.0740	-0.1517	1.0000

Thus, basic assumptions of the linear regression model seem not to be violated. Apart from model violations, the low number of observations (77) could be a reason for the insignificance of *EDU.* Most authors suggest that the number of observations should be at least 10 to 20 larger than the number of variables (e.g. Peduzzi et al., 1996). Another reason could be that EDU only differentiates between quantitative and non-quantitative education. Managers with a background in business and economics, which can be situated between quantitative and qualitative fields of study, are grouped together with traditionally qualitative subjects such as the humanities. This can also dilute differences.

If one disregards the fact that EDU is not statistically significant, the regression shows that the observed differences in levels of overconfidence remain, even after controlling for factors known to influence overconfidence. This means that in the analyzed sample of CEOs of the largest German companies, systematic differences in levels of overconfidence can be observed that seem to stem from a factor which has not previously been shown to affect overconfidence: the major field of study in an individual's educational background. On top of these empirical findings, there is also experimental evidence supporting this connection, which I will present in the following section.

5.2 Experimental Evidence

Many studies on the topic of overconfidence investigate the impact of education on overconfident behavior. Despite awareness of the fact that education influences the level of overconfidence to my knowledge, there is only one study that differentiates between participants that were educated in different academic fields. This series of experiments conducted by Schulz and Thöni (2011) serves at this point as experimental evidence for my hypothesis of a relationship between an individual's field of study and proneness to overconfidence.

5.2.1 Data

Schulz and Thöni obtained their data from questionnaires, which were distributed among subjects at the end of an unrelated experiment. In the questionnaire, the subjects were asked to guess the years in which five historical events happened. In different sessions, the authors varied the difficulty of questions, subject areas and group sizes. Subjects, who attended the same session and were therefore compared to each other, always answered the exact same questions and were told the size of their benchmark group beforehand. Subjects received payment depending on their performance as defined by the deviations of the subjects' answers from the correct years. For each question, subjects could earn 2 Swiss Francs for a correct answer. This sum was reduced by 0.2 Francs for each year that their answer deviated from the correct year up to a maximum of ten years. Participants were, moreover, asked to guess their performance-based rank relative to their group, which gave them the possibility to earn an additional 5 Francs if their guess was correct.

The study was conducted with undergraduate students from the University of Zurich and the University of St. Gallen over a period of 5 years between 2005 and 2010. A total of 391 students participated in the study. At the University of Zurich, students start their studies by immediately choosing their subject of study, whereas students at the University of St. Gallen start with an "assessment year" of general studies in the fields of business, economics, and law. During this assessment year, students have a very limited choice of subjects and may only chose between mathematical and law track. By the end of the assessment year, students chose what degree they wish to pursue and transfer to the respective program. This means that the major field of study that researchers recorded as part of personal data consists, for first-year students from the University of St. Gallen, of the intended choice rather than the actual major.

As a measure of overconfidence, Schulz and Thöni calculated the difference between the guessed rank of a subject and his or her true rank. A negative difference therefore means that a subject underestimated his or her performance, while a positive difference would indicate overconfidence. The results of this misplacement are presented below.

5.2.2 Results

Schulz and Thöni discovered that, rather less surprisingly, on average, students overestimate their rank and, therefore, are overconfident. Defining the confidence level of a person to be the number of ranks she overestimates (positive number) or underestimates (negative number) her true rank in the guessing game, the average as well as the median of confidence levels is significantly higher than zero.

Figure 2: Distribution of Confidence Levels

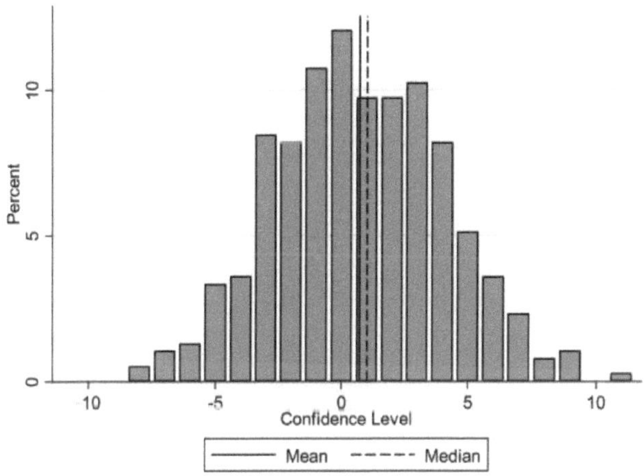

Source: Schulz and Thöni (2011)

More strikingly, there are differences in the levels of confidence between students of different subjects:

Figure 3: Mean Confidence Levels by Field of Studies

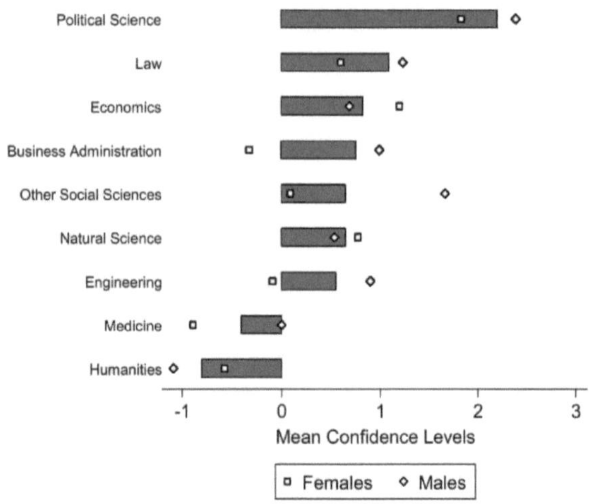

Source: Schulz and Thöni (2011)

While students of political science overestimate themselves by more than two ranks on average, students of the humanities underestimate their performance by nearly one rank. Except for the two groups that on average underestimate themselves, that is students of medicine and humanities, the results support the initial hypothesis and are consistent with the empirical findings presented above. While students of rather qualitative subjects, such as political science and law, exhibit the highest levels of overconfidence, students with a rather quantitative background like natural sciences or engineering are less overconfident. As for medical students, whose education consists for a large part of natural sciences, it is not surprising that they are found at the lower end of the table with respect to overconfidence, even though their confidence levels are even lower than one might expect. However, what is rather striking is that students of the humanities, who might be expected to exhibit levels of overconfidence similar to political science students, are actually the ones who are most under-confident about their performance. Despite the qualitative nature of their education, they exhibit the least (over-)confidence.

5.3 Discussion

The empirical data as well as the experimental findings presented in this chapter both indicate that an individual's proneness to overconfidence is linked to the major field of study. Both the example, of German CEOs and the one of Swiss university students, suggest that individuals with a rather quantitative education exhibit lower overconfidence than individuals with a qualitative education. Of course, the significance of this evidence should not be overstated.

In the example of CEOs, the standard deviation of overconfidence levels is relatively high (around 30% of the scores), calling into question the reliability of the data. This could be due to the low number of observations in the data set which also reduces the statistical significance of differences in overconfidence. Furthermore, the key words for the analysis of press portrayal were chosen relatively arbitrarily. It might be that he results will be different if other key words are chosen.

However, one also has to bear in mind that all subjects from the data set are leaders of internationally operating companies. Literature on promotion of successful employees suggests that overconfident individuals are most likely to advance this far up the ranks in a company. Therefore, even small differences in (over-)confidence between managers of such a high level could denote significant differences for individuals with lower absolute levels of overconfidence.

Schulz and Thöni's data is based on the intended choice of major for students at St. Gallen. These statements do not necessarily match the students' final decisions. Moreover, students of the humanities being the least overconfident in their rank estimation does not fit at all into the proposed logic that qualitatively educated individuals are more overconfident than quantitatively educated ones.

What both studies have in common is that they do not allow for any conclusions about whether the field of education impacts overconfidence or whether education and overconfidence are linked in some other way. Overconfident by nature individuals might, for example, prefer certain university programs, such as political sciences, while underconfident individuals are more drawn towards natural sciences and other quantitative subjects. Schulz and Thöni's finding that differences in levels of overconfidence can be observed at a relatively early stage of higher education would support this explanation.

Nevertheless, both pieces of evidence indicate independently from each other that the field of studies in higher education and a person's level of overconfidence are linked. This allows for the formulation of a working hypothesis: if overconfidence is linked to a person's education, then people from a quantitative field like mathematics or natural sciences will be less prone to overconfidence than those from qualitative fields like humanities or law. The evidence presented in this chapter does not allow for accepting or rejecting this hypothesis but it certainly motivates further investigation.

6 Dual Reasoning and Overconfidence

In this chapter, I will argue that systematic differences in overconfidence based on differences in education and training as suggested by the evidence presented in the previous chapter is consistent with the theory of human dual process reasoning. After presenting the general concept of dual reasoning, I will discuss what impact differences in education and training can have on ways of thinking and how style of thought influences decision making. I will show that, within the framework of dual process reasoning, differences in overconfidence can arise from different mind-sets of people acquired through their education and training.

6.1 Concept of Dual Reasoning

The notion of a dualist distinction between human reasoning systems can be traced back to the work of William James and Sigmund Freud (Osman, 2004). Both psychologists claimed that human reasoning could manifest itself in two distinct systems of thought, one being associative and unconscious while the other is analytical, rational, and conscious. Especially over the last 30 years, many researchers have come forward with their own versions of this basic idea.

One of the earlier papers is by Schneider and Shiffrin (1977a). These researchers conducted a series of attention experiments in order to study how people process information. Subjects were shown frames of characters, while being asked to search for the occurrence of certain characters they held in short-term memory. The experiments were designed in such a way that they consisted of two distinct tasks. In a first detection task, subjects simply had to judge whether a certain character had been shown to them or not. In a second search task, subjects had to actively search for a target character in a frame. The researchers found that the accuracy of subjects in the detection tasks hardly showed any "size effects", i.e. accuracy did not decrease significantly with an increasing number of characters per frame or total number of frames presented. In contrast to this, the time the subjects needed for the search tasks seemed to depend heavily upon the "load" of the frame. To explain this observed difference between detection and search, Schneider and Shiffrin proposed a dual model of information processing, consisting of automatic detection and controlled processing. According to them, automatic detection uses sequences that do not require attention and works independently of short-term memory, meaning that "size", i.e. the number of elements in a detection task, does not influence accuracy. Controlled processing, however, is used for search tasks, requires attention, and uses short-term memory which is why adding more distractions or elements to be searched for increases time spent on the task.

While most of the work on dual reasoning disagrees on technical details concerning how the two systems are used, such as whether they are exclusive, parallel, or sequential, most researchers agree that two distinct reasoning systems exist. As a consequence, the different traits attributed to the two systems are consistent with each other.[10] The following table gives an overview of the labels attached to the two distinct systems, using the terminology of "System 1" and "System 2" introduced by Stanovic (1999) and used in the majority of literature ever since:

Table 4: Labels Attached to Reasoning Systems

References	System 1	System 2
Fodor (1983, 2001)	Input modules	Higher cognition
Schneider & Schiffrin (1977)	Automatic	Controlled
Epstein (1994), Epstein & Pacini (1999)	Experiential	Rational
Chaiken (1980), Chen & Chaiken (1999)	Heuristic	Systematic
Reber (1993), Evans & Over (1996)	Implicit, tacit	Explicit
Evans (1989, 2006)	Heuristic	Analytic
Sloman (1996), Smith & DeCoster (2000)	Associative	Rule based
Hammond (1996)	Intuitive	Analytic
Stanovich (1999, 2004)	System 1 (TASS)	System 2 (Analytic)
Nisbett et al. (2001)	Holistic	Analytic
Wilson (2002)	Adaptive unconscious	Conscious
Lieberman (2003)	Reflexive	Reflective
Toates (2006)	Stimulus bound	Higher order
Strack & Deustch (2004)	Impulsive	Reflective

Source: Evans (2008)

While most work focuses on the conception of such dualist models of reasoning and the attempt to assign observed human behavior to one of the reasoning systems, few researchers

[10] See Evans (2008) for a review of concepts

tried to discover neuro-physiological evidence for dual reasoning. One such study is Goel et al. (2000), in which the authors used functional magnetic resonance imaging (fMRI) to show which brain areas are active during different reasoning processes. Goel et al. measured subjects' brain activity during syllogistic reasoning tasks with and without conventional semantic sense. The tasks with semantic sense followed the style of "all dogs are pets; all pets are furry; all dogs are furry", while the logically equivalent tasks without semantic sense followed the style of "all A are B; all B are C; all A are C". The researchers discovered that for the different tasks, subjects used two dissociable neurological networks in their brains. This supports the notion that humans do not only process information and reason in two different ways, but they do so by using neurologically distinguishable cognitive systems.

6.2 Differences in Reasoning

According to the concept of dual reasoning, all individuals generally make use of both systems. However, which system is used in what situation seems to depend upon the individual person. This point is critical for the subsequent argument, and, therefore, I will first present evidence for individual differences in the usage of the two reasoning systems and then cite literature on how and when this individual use may alter.

A common psychological experiment for studying differences in reasoning is the Wason selection task (Wason, 1968). Cognitive psychologist Peter Cathcart Wason conducted an experiment in which he placed four cards on a table. The cards had "D", "3", "B", and "7" printed on them. Subjects were told that every card had a letter on one side and a number on the other side. Furthermore, the subjects were told that "If there is a D on one side of a card, then there is a 3 on the other side". The task was to decide, for each of the four cards, whether turning it around and seeing the number or letter on the other side would enable them to answer whether the sentence was true or false. Wason discovered that almost all subjects correctly decided to turn over the "D" -card, however, about 65% decided to check the "3" -card, which was wrong, because the sentence did not rule out that a card with a letter other than "D" could also have a "3" on the other side. Only a few subjects chose to turn over the "7" card, which would have been correct since a "D" on the other side of this card could have proven the sentence wrong.

Variations of this original design have been widely used to study reasoning and to find explanations for the poor performance noted by Wason. One variation used for this purpose is to put Wason's abstract selection task into a more realistic or social context. Griggs and Cox

(1982) repeated Wason's experiment, giving their subjects two tasks. While the first one was the standard Wason task, the second task put the selection into a thematic context. Instead of using abstract letters and numbers, the researchers wrote "Drinking beer", "Drinking coke", "16 years of age" and "22 years of age" on the cards and changed the control sentence to "If a person is drinking beer, then the person must be over 19 years of age". This way the general form of both tasks remained "p", "not-p", "q", "not-q" with the control sentence "If p then q" as in Wason's design. Griggs and Cox found that subjects performed far better on the drinking-age problem than on the abstract task.

6.2.1 Fixed Factors

Stanovic and West (1998) proposed a dual-reasoning explanation for this significantly better performance of subjects when the selection task is put into a thematic or social context. According to them, the correct solution of an abstract selection task requires the use of analytical System 2 thinking and thus a higher cognitive ability. Correctly solving the selection task when it is put in a social context, however, can be done using heuristics and previous experience, which are associated with System 1 and equally well-employed by people regardless of other cognitive characteristics. This explanation is supported by the authors' experimental finding that performance on the abstract selection task is highly correlated with the subjects' SAT scores and general intelligence, while there is no such correlation when the selection task is presented in a thematic context. Thus, Stanovic and West discovered that, in comparable settings, some people (in their case those with higher cognitive abilities) rather make use of System 2 thinking while others might rather use System 1 thinking.

Evans (2003) shows that, on top of general intelligence, working-memory capacity also has an influence upon the use of cognitive systems. According to the author, System 2 uses working memory as a resource. Smaller working-memory capacity thus limits System 2 use. It is debated to what extent working memory can be extended through training and to what extent it is fixed and underlies general intelligence.[11] If one regards general intelligence and working-memory capacity as relatively stable, this raises the question of what other possible variables, apart from general intelligence and working-memory, affect people's use of the distinct reasoning systems.

---

[11] See for example Conway et al. (2003) and Jaeggi et al. (2008).

6.2.2 Trainability

In Houdé et al. (2000) the authors tested whether the performance of subjects on a deductive logic task could be enhanced by bias-inhibition training. During their experiment, the authors additionally used positron emission tomography (PET) to see what, if any, effects such training had on brain activity. When the subjects initially faced a task similar to the Wason selection task they performed similar to Wason's original results and the results of other replicating studies: most subjects came to a wrong solution by falling prey to an effect called matching bias. This bias describes people's tendency to respond to elements in a selection task, which appeared in the conditional of the task. In the example of Wason, subjects would choose "p" and "q" because the conditional sentence was "If p then q" instead of the correct answer "p" and "not-q".[12] Following an initial performance test, subjects were made aware of them falling prey to a bias and instructed on how to avoid matching bias by considering every element of the selection task carefully and not deciding intuitively. After this training, subjects solved a selection task similar to the first one. The authors found that not only had the training significantly enhanced subjects' performance, but, according to the PET scans, the brain regions used by subjects for reasoning had changed. The authors concluded that, because of the training, the subjects' brain activity had shifted from areas primarily associated with perception to those associated with logic. In the context of dual reasoning, the subjects had learned to use System 2 thinking on a task they originally solved incorrectly by using System 1 thinking.

The effect of particular training on the use of reasoning systems is also studied by Inglis and Simpson (2004). They compared the performance of mathematicians and historians on a standard Wason selection task and found that, even though both groups had relatively low success rates, the mathematicians still performed significantly better. In an attempt to explain the better performance of mathematicians, the authors compared the errors made by the different groups and found systematic differences. While the historians followed a behavioral pattern associated with matching bias, the mathematicians did not make this error. Inglis and Simpson attribute this to the importance of error checking in mathematical education. The authors suggest that the initial and intuitive choice of the mathematicians is also "p" and "not-q" but, in contrast to non-mathematicians they are better trained to critically rethink their initial choice and realize that checking "not-q" is unnecessary. This is supported by the fact

[12] See Evans (1998) for a thorough review.

that the error most often made by subjects in the mathematicians group is checking only "p". If the intuitive initial choice is associated with System 1 thinking, while critically rethinking the first choice is associated with System 2, the authors' results suggest that mathematically-trained individuals use System 2 thinking more often and, therefore, perform better on cognitive tasks than non-mathematicians.

6.2.3 Manipulability

One possible way to manipulate a subject's choice of reasoning systems is presented in a study on the interaction between affect and cognition by Shiv and Fedorikhin (1999). These researchers constructed an experimental design, in which subjects had to choose between fruit salad and a piece of chocolate cake as a snack while walking from one room to another room across the hall. The subjects were divided into two groups. Subjects from the first group were asked to memorize a two-digit number, while subjects from the second group had to memorize a seven-digit number. The only difference between subject groups was the length of the number they had to memorize before making the decision. Only 41% of the subjects from the first group chose the chocolate cake as compared to 63% of subjects in the second group. Thus, the vast majority of the first group chose the fruit salad, and most subjects from the second group preferred the cakes. The authors attribute this difference in choice to different reasoning employed by the subjects, depending on how much working memory was available to them. When being asked to memorize only two digits, first-group subjects' choice was driven by cognition. This resulted in the more level-headed choice to eat the healthy fruit salad, which was superior to the cake on the cognitive dimension but inferior on the affective dimension. Subjects from the second group had to remember seven digits, which fully occupied their working memory. Under this constraint of resources, subjects' choice was rather driven by affect and most chose the snack superior on this dimension, namely the cake.

As discussed in chapter 6.2.1, the availability of working memory is crucial for System 2 thinking. If the fruit salad is seen as a healthy and rational choice and the chocolate cake as an impulsive and hasty choice, the results of Shiv and Fedorikhin are consistent with the concept of dual reasoning. Subjects from the first group made their choice regarding their snack using, at least in part, System 2. Subjects from the second group were manipulated by limiting their working memory and, therefore, their System 2 thinking was restrained. Thus the subjects in the second group had to decide using mainly System 1, which consequently led them to choose the unhealthy chocolate cake. The experiment by Shiv and Fedorikhin shows that choice of reasoning systems is not only trainable but also easily manipulated.

6.3 Reasoning Systems and Overconfidence

For abstract Wason selection task, the use of System 2 thinking results in a correct solution, whereas using heuristic System 1 come to a biased and incorrect solution. This example again shows that the two systems of reasoning presented above are quite different in their functioning. As a consequence, an individual can come to different conclusions, depending on which of the two systems she uses in a particular situation. If the distinct use of reasoning systems has an influence on an individual's performance on certain tasks, this raises the question of whether it also influences belief about her information and performance.

As discussed in chapter 3.1, many researchers seek an explanation for why people are overconfident in information processing. Koriat et al. (1980), Klayman and Ha (1989), as well as McKenzie (1997) see a main reason for overconfidence in people's tendency to draw conclusions quickly and neglect contradictory evidence. One difference between System 1 and System 2 thinking is the use of heuristics rather than analytical thinking. One could, therefore, say that System 1 thinking leads to quick conclusions without proper consideration of counterarguments, while System 2 promotes prudent reasoning and pondering various kinds of information.

When a person is forced to predict an outcome or assess her own performance, the result is influenced by reasoning processes. When using System 1, the person thinks intuitively and reflexively, which decreases accuracy of judgment on the one hand and hampers critical reflection of accuracy on the other hand. This combination of low accuracy and limited possibility of critical reflection can be expected to foster overconfidence. Contrary to this, System 2, which is associated with abstract and logical thinking, increases accuracy through systematic and analytical reasoning. At the same time, it facilitates critical reflection by slow, sequential, and rule-based thought processes. A person can thus be expected to exhibit more overconfidence when using System 1 and less overconfidence when using System 2.

Drawing a connection between the concept of dual reasoning and cognitive biases such as overconfidence is nothing new. Daniel Kahneman brings forth a very similar argument in his book *Thinking, Fast and Slow* (2011) in a popular scientific way. However, to my knowledge, neither Kahneman himself nor any other author has elaborated on this idea in a scholarly publication to this time. Thus, for this link in my chain of argument, no scholarly evidence is available. That is the reason why, in chapter 7, I will come back to the relationship between cognitive systems and overconfidence and propose an experimental design that could test my claim.

6.4 Differences in Training and Overconfidence

In the preceding three sections, three important components of the framework of dual reasoning have been discussed. On the one hand, I discussed how the use of reasoning systems differs among individuals and where the development of System 2 thinking seems to be susceptible to influence by training and education. On the other hand, I presented studies that suggest that a person's judgment is strongly influenced by whether she uses reflexive and intuitive System 1 or reflective and analytical System 2 thinking in her reasoning. Combining these two components leads to the idea that individuals with different training and/or educational backgrounds are likely to reason and judge in different ways, because, due to differences in training, they make distinct usage of the two reasoning systems. It is conceivable that, when faced with the same situation, a person who was predominantly trained to think reflectively and analytically might use System 2 thinking thus and come to a different conclusion than a person who mostly thinks reflexively and impulsively.

As a third component, I argued that the use of intuitive and heuristic System 1 thinking fosters overconfidence, while system 2 thinking, that allows more reflective and critical thinking, hampers it. Adding this component to the chain forms the central proposition of this study: different training can lead to distinct uses of the two systems of reasoning and ultimately foster or hamper overconfidence. Alternatively, the differences in levels of overconfidence observed between individuals with different educational backgrounds can be explained by the different training they received during their education which led to different usage of reasoning systems.

People who have received a rather quantitative education and extensive mathematical training (e.g. mathematicians and physicists) are often faced with situations in their education in which intuitive and heuristic thinking leads to wrong conclusions or does not help at all. They are, instead, trained to think analytically and taught to abstract rather than contextualize, which goes hand-in-hand with the use of System 2. Following this prior training, they are better able to reflect on their own judgments and less prone to heuristic biases than individuals with a rather qualitative background.

Previous research on how education influences overconfidence has been confined to duration and quality by investigating the relation between extent of education and level of overconfidence. This paper, I have shown that a different aspect of education not studied yet might be equally important, namely the major field of study in an individual's educational background. Instead of asking, „are better educated individuals more or less prone to overconfidence?“, I therefore ask, „are individuals who have been trained to think more mathematically and analytically, more or less prone to overconfidence?“

7 Experimental Approach

In chapter 6, I argued that System 1 thinking fosters overconfidence while System 2 thinking hampers it. This idea is critical for my chain of argument concerning the influence of the nature of an individual's education on overconfidence. Based on research from both fields, that is overconfidence and dual reasoning, the connection established in chapter 6.4 seems plausible. However, for this crucial step, no direct supporting evidence from other studies exists because no study presently available to me puts these two concepts into relation. Therefore, this claim should be tested in order to support my hypothesis. In the following section, I suggest an experiment to test this claim.

7.1 Hypothesis

To conduct an experiment, a testable hypothesis needs to be formulated. Again, the underlying notion to be supported or weakened by experimental evidence is that differences in overconfidence between individuals can be explained by distinct uses of reasoning systems as described by the theory of dual process reasoning. Consequently, the general hypothesis is that distinct uses of reasoning systems affect proneness to overconfidence. If the results of the motivating evidence from chapter 5 and the explanation why reasoning and overconfidence could be connected from chapter 6.4 are taken into account, the hypothesis can be refined by adding directionality: overconfidence should be higher when System 1 is used. Accordingly, the hypothesis to be examined is:

H_1: *If overconfidence is related to the use of reasoning systems, then people who use System 1 thinking will exhibit higher levels of overconfidence than those using System 2 thinking in the same reasoning process.*

Consequently, the null hypothesis that is tested and sought to be rejected is:

H_0: *Overconfidence is not related to the use of reasoning systems; therefore there will be no significant difference in the level of overconfidence between people who use System 1 and people who use System 2 thinking in a reasoning process.*

7.2 Preliminary Considerations

In order to test the hypothesis formulated above, two preliminary considerations need to be taken into account: firstly, what measure of overconfidence could be used, and, secondly, how a subject's use of reasoning systems could be manipulated.

Concerning the measurement of overconfidence, validity of overconfidence measure is an important aspect. Klayman et al. (1999) point at the problem, that, when measuring overconfidence, purely statistical effects are often confounded with the psychological effect to be measured. The authors show that subjects exhibit significantly higher levels of overconfidence when asked for confidence intervals than when asked to answer two-choice questions. This finding is consistent with the conclusion that miscalibration results from unsystematic error rather than from systematic overconfidence bias. This stresses the importance of distinguishing between mere inability to cope with a given task and a systematically biased belief about the accuracy of one's performance.

To measure overconfidence, the widely-used method of interval estimation seems convenient. This method consists of asking subjects to give, for example, a 90%-confidence interval in which they believe an unknown exogenous variable, such as the year in which a historical event happened, lies. As studies by Soll and Klayman (2004) and Ben-David et al. (2006) show, variables fall constantly less than X% of the time into subjects' X%-confidence intervals, which indicates overconfidence. It has to be kept in mind that the overconfidence variable to be measured here is not subjects' lack of knowledge of the variable's true value, but their unawareness of their knowledge deficit. To be able to differentiate between such mistakes of misestimation and overconfidence, an incentive scheme as proposed by Krawczyk (2011) can be used. The idea behind an incentive scheme is not just to ask subjects for their confidence intervals but to incentivize them based on whether their reported range contains the true value and penalize them the larger their reported range becomes. Thus, as Krawczyk proposes, one could ask subjects to estimate the distance in kilometers between pairs of major European cities and report their 90%-confidence interval. The subjects would receive a fixed payment every time the true value fell into their reported interval and be charged a small amount for every kilometer of their reported range. In this setting one could use the distance between the true value and the middle of the subject's reported interval every time the true value fell outside the interval as a measure of overconfidence.

To manipulate choice of reasoning systems, the method introduced by Gilbert et al. (1988) and used in the experiment by Shiv and Fedorikhin (1999) described in chapter 6.2.3 can be used. Subjects are kept busy by having to memorize information, e. g. a seven-digit number like in the experiment by Shiv and Fedorkhin. This occupies subjects' working memory. As discussed in chapter 6.2.1, the use of System 2 requires working memory. Insufficient resources lead to the use of System 1 in situations where subjects would normally have used System 2. To contrast System 1 and System 2 thinking, one group of subjects is asked to memorize a seven-digit number before the range-estimation task and incentivized by a fixed payment if the subject correctly remembers the number at the end of the experiment.

7.3 Experimental Setup

In order to support or weaken my hypothesis overconfidence should be compared between two groups of subjects, with one group predominantly using System 1 and the other group using System 2 while overconfidence is being measured. Based on the preliminary considerations discussed above, the experiment could be designed as follows:

The subjects are randomly assigned to one of two equal groups. Subjects from both groups are told that they will be presented with 20 pairs of major European cities. For each pair, they will have to estimate the distance between the two cities by reporting an interval for which they are 90% sure that it contains the true value. Subjects are also told that they will receive 500 points every time their reported range contains the correct distance and that they have to pay 1 point for every kilometer of their range. These proposed values can be manipulated depending on which cities and distances are chosen and, consequently, how precise the subjects' estimates can be expected to be. Schlag and van der Weele (2009) propose quantitative criteria for efficient scoring rules for the case that boundary values between which the unknown variable can lie are known. Depending on the city pairs used and whether subjects are given a hint like "all cities in this task have a distance between 1,000 and 3,000 kilometers", this efficiency rule could be used. Moreover, the conversion factor of points into real money can be varied depending on how long the experiment takes and what payment is expected by subjects in order to be effectively motivated to participate in the experiment.

After the explanation of the task and the incentive/penalty system, subjects are presented 20 city pairs one after another and asked to report their 90% confidence intervals for the distances without receiving any feedback. Using the subjects' reported intervals, a proxy for the overconfidence in both groups can be calculated as described in 7.2. If the groups are equal and sufficiently large, the calculated level of overconfidence should be equal.

After the first round, subjects from both groups are told that they are going to repeat the game, however, this time they will have to memorize a certain number during the game. Subjects from group 1 are given a randomly drawn two-digit number and told, that they will receive a payment of 5 Swiss Francs if they remember this number at the end of the experiment. Subjects from group 2 are given a seven-digit number and promised 5 Swiss Francs if they still remember it by the end of the treatment. After being given some time to memorize the numbers, the treatment as described above is repeated and subjects have to again report confidence intervals for distances between 20 (different) pairs of cities.

Following the last pair, the subjects are told how much they have earned during the two games and asked to recall the number they have been told at the beginning of the second part of the experiment. Depending on whether they correctly remembered their number, their payoff is increased.

As in the first part of the experiment overconfidence scores for subjects in both groups are calculated. If the overconfidence of group 1 is statistically significantly higher than group 2's score, the null hypothesis H_0 can be rejected and H_1 accepted instead. In that case, the experiment would support the claim that distinct use of reasoning systems affects the level of overconfidence.

7.4 Additional Testing

Another important element in my chain of argument in chapter 6.4 is the idea that the use of reasoning systems is trained during an individual's education. This idea was built on the finding of Houdé et al. (2000) that, through special training, the use of reasoning systems in a certain task could be affected as well. It is also supported by the finding of Inglis and Simpson (2004) that the reasoning exhibited by mathematicians is consistent with the points emphasized most during mathematical education. Both papers indicate the above mentioned relationship but do not directly prove it. Even if the distinct use of reasoning systems is trainable, the differences in reasoning displayed by differently educated individuals could be a spurious correlation. It is imaginable that people who predominantly use System 2 and are less overconfident by nature, are also more prone to choosing an analytical and more quantitative career. At the same time, individuals who mostly use System 1, are creative rather than analytical, and possibly overconfident by nature, might be attracted to qualitative fields like arts or humanities.

This calls for further investigation into which differences in overconfidence levels already exist before higher education and to what extent different training influences these differences. For this to be accurately determined, one would ideally measure overconfidence of students of different subjects at different points in their studies. Most importantly, one would compare overconfidence levels of students just after they entered university to those of students right before graduation. This would allow researchers to see whether systematic differences exist already after secondary school when no significant differentiation in training has taken place yet. Alternatively, one might discover that overconfidence levels of quantitatively and qualitatively educated students drift apart as the hypothesis put forward in this study suggests.

7.5 Interpretation of Results

If the points made by this paper can be supported by evidence, as proposed in the last two sections, this would have numerous implications for professional practice. As discussed in chapter 4.2, overconfidence plays an important role in security trading. Overconfident individuals execute too many trades that lead to worse performance. Quantitatively educated individuals, like mathematicians or physicists, could, however, be expected to act in a more level-headed and less overconfident manner and would, therefore, be well-suited for professional trader positions. More generally speaking, if the argument of this paper is taken to its logical conclusion, the suitability for particular tasks and jobs could be determined not only by professional knowledge and experience but also partially by a person's mindset formed during her education.

Besides general suitability, the trainability of uses of reasoning systems could also be utilized for the changing responsibilities of managers. At some point in their careers, managers advance to positions where the direct leadership of employees is no longer their main task, and strategic planning and decision making become more important. At this point, System 1 thinking, which goes hand-in-hand with higher overconfidence and which has up until this advancement, been beneficial in terms of employee motivation and leadership, becomes hindering. To address this change in requirements special training in formal logic and bias-inhibition techniques could be conducted to enhance the use of System 2 instead of System 1.

A more general implication would be the additional information, which investors, supervisors or competitors could get about a manager solely by getting to know her educational background. In a principal-agent setting, such as a board of supervisors appointing a new CEO, the principal could make inferences about individual overconfidence and, therefore, the agent's tendencies. This would enable the principal to design a contract with incentives more specifically designed to elicit optimum performance from that particular agent. Investors would have additional information for evaluating a manager's forecasts, and the market would be able to assess the information more adequately. Moreover, the market could punish a company that appoints a CEO with a strong qualitative education based solely on the presumption that a qualitatively educated CEO will act in an overconfident manner and make unfavorable decisions for the company.

8 Conclusion

In this study, I investigated the question whether the major field of an individual's education can influence proneness to overconfidence. Before concluding with an overview of what the ideas developed in this paper could mean for further research, I summarize my arguments and results in the following section.

8.1 Summary

As a basis, I provided a literature review on overconfidence, including research on the general concept, sources of this bias, and implications for business and economics. I then presented experimental and empirical results that indicated systematic differences in the levels of overconfidence between individuals with different educational backgrounds, which could not be properly explained by factors known to influence overconfidence. In both pieces of evidence, individuals with a quantitative education, for example in mathematics or physics, exhibited less overconfidence than individuals with a more qualitative education, such as in law or the humanities. Based on this, I formulated the working hypothesis that a quantitative education reduces an individual's proneness to overconfidence while a qualitative education fosters it.

In order to corroborate this hypothesis, I introduced the theory of dual process reasoning and argued that my working hypothesis is consistent with this psychological framework. According to dual reasoning theory, humans use two functionally and physiologically distinct cognitive systems of reasoning. While the first system [System 1] is fast, impulsive, context-bound, and makes use of heuristics, the second system [System 2] is slow and resource consuming, but also analytical and responsible for what is termed rational thinking. Using these labels attached to the systems by various research, I argued that System 1 fosters overconfidence through the use of heuristics, while System 2 hampers it allowing for critical reflection and analytical thinking. To relate this to education, I cited psychological literature showing that the distinct use of the reasoning systems is trainable. Furthermore, I presented a study suggesting that individuals with mathematical training seem to predominantly use System 2 because of the emphasis on analytical and abstract thinking as well as on critical reflection during higher mathematical education. Building on this, I formulated the explanatory approach that through different educational styles individuals are trained to make distinct use of reasoning systems and are, therefore, dissimilarly prone to overconfidence.

Since there seems to be no direct evidence from previous research supporting the claim that System 1 thinking fosters overconfidence while System 2 hampers it, I proposed an experimental design in which this claim could be tested. Furthermore, I suggested a survey measuring overconfidence of individuals at various points in their studies. This would allow researchers to investigate whether differences in overconfidence are, indeed, formed during higher education, or whether individuals who are more prone to overconfidence by nature choose predominantly qualitative fields while those less prone prefer quantitative subjects.

8.2 Outlook

Even if the link between education and the distinct use of reasoning systems is shown not to hold when taken as a whole, the suggestion that overconfidence is related to dual reasoning is still innovative and invites for further research. The explanatory approach, using dual process reasoning theory, could also be expanded to other cognitive biases. For example, it could be explored whether the use of System 2 generally hampers cognitive biases, in which case biased behavior could be reduced by enhancing System 2 use. If this were true then one could theoretically measure constructs like an individual's "general proneness to cognitive biases" by exploring what regions of the brain are used predominantly and to which reasoning system they correspond.

The starting point of this paper was to find possible explanations for systematic differences in levels of overconfidence observed in an experiment and found in an empirical data set. However, the ideas evolved in the course of investigation go much further, and reveal, once again, the important role that cognitive psychology plays in behavioral economics and finance. While psychological concepts have been widely used to explain economic behavior, the chain of neuro-physiological brain activity, psychological processes and their consequences for economic behavior is rarely treated as the unified system that it is. This paper certainly recommends further thinking in this direction using a holistic approach.

9 References

Alicke, M. D., Govorun, O. (2005). The Better-Than-Average Effect. In: M. D. Alicke, D. A. Dunning, J. I. Krueger, eds. *The Self in Social Judgment. Studies in self and identity*. New York, N. Y.: Psychology Press, 2005, pp. 85–106).

Allan, L. G., Jenkins, H. M. (1980). The Judgment of Contingency and the Nature of the Response Alternatives. *Canadian Journal of Psychology, 34,* 1–11.

Allen, W. D., Evans, D. A. (2005). Bidding and Overconfidence in Experimental Financial Markets. *Journal of Behavioral Finance, 6 (3)*, 108–120.

Almazan, A., De Motta, A., Titman, S. (2007). Firm Location and the Creation and Utilization of Human Capital. *Review of Economic Studies, 74 (4),* 1305–1327.

Alpert, M., Raiffa, H. (1982). A Progress Report on the Training of Probability Assessors. In: D. Kahneman, P. Slavic, L A. Tversky, eds. *Judgment under uncertainty: Heuristics and biases*. Cambridge, England: Cambridge Univ. Press, 1982, pp. 294–305.

Baker, L. A., Emery, R. E. (1993). When Every Relationship Is above Average: Perceptions and Expectations of Divorce at the Time of Marriage. *Law and Human Behavior, 17 (4),* 439–450.

Barberis, N., Thaler, R. (2003). A Survey of Behavioral Finance. In: G. M. Constantinides, M. Harris, R. Stulz, eds. *Handbook of the Economics of Finance*. Amsterdam: Elsevier, 2003, pp. 1052–1114.

Barber, B. M., Odean, T. (2001). Boys will be boys: Gender, overconfidence, and common stock investment, *Quarterly Journal of Economics, 116 (1),* 261–292.

Barros, L. A. B. de C., A Di M. da Silveira. (2008). Overconfidence, Managerial Optimism and the Determinants of Capital Structure. *Brazilian Review of Finance, 6 (3),* 293–334.

Ben-David, I., Graham, J. R., Harvey, C. R. (2010). Managerial Miscalibration (Working Paper No. 16215). Retrieved from National Bureau of Economic Research website: http://www.nber.org/papers/w16215.

Benos, A. V. (1998). Overconfident Speculators in Call Markets: Trade Patterns and Survival. *Journal of Financial Markets, 1,* 353–383.

Bernardo, A. E., Welch, I. (2001). On the Evolution of Overconfidence and Entrepreneurs. *Journal of Economics and Management Strategy, 10 (3),* 301–330.

Bertrand, M., Schoar, A. (2003). *Managing with Style: The Effect of Managers on Firm Policies. Quarterly Journal of Economics, 118 (4),* 1169–1208.

Billett, M. T., Qian, Y. (2008). Are Overconfident Managers Born or Made? Evidence of Self-Attribution Bias from Frequent Acquirers. *Management Science, 54 (6),* 1037–1051.

Blanton, H., Pelham, B. W., DeHart, T., Carvallo, M. (2001). Overconfidence as Dissonance Reduction. *Journal of Experimental Social Psychology, 37,* 373–385.

Bornstein, B. H., Zickafoose, D. J. (1999). I Know I Know It, I Know I Saw It“: The Stability of the Confidence-Accuracy Relationship Across Domains. *Journal of Experimental Psychology: Applied, 5 (1),* 76–88.

Brenner, L. A., Koehler, D. J., Liberman, V., Tversky, A. (1996). Overconfidence in Probability and Frequency Judgments: A Critical Examination. *Organizational Behavior and Human Decision Processes, 65 (3),* 212–219.

Budescu, D. V., Wallsten, T. S., Wu, W. T. (1997). On the Importance of Random Error in the Study of Probability Judgment. Part II: Applying the Stochastic Judgment Model to Detect Systematic Trends. *Journal of Behavioral Decision Making 10 (3),* 173–188.

Camerer, C. F., Lovallo, D. (1999). Overconfidence and Excess Entry: An Experimental Approach. *American Economic Review, 89 (1).* 306–318.

Cooper, A. C., Woo, C. Y., Dunkelberg, W. C. (1988). Entrepreneurs' perceived chances for success. *Journal of Business Venturing, 3 (2),* 97–108.

Conway, A. R., Kane, M. J., Engle R. W., (2003). Working memory capacity and its relation to general intelligence. *Trends in Cognitive Sciences 7 (12)*, 547–552.

Daniel, K. D., Hirshleifer, D., Subrahmanyam, A. (2001). Overconfidence, Arbitrage, and Equilibrium Asset Pricing. *Journal of Finance, 56 (3),* 921–965.

DeLong, B. J., Shleifer, A., Summers, L. H., Waldmann, R. (1990). Noise Trader Risk in Financial Markets. Journal of Political Economy, 98 (4) 703–738.

De Bondt, W., Thaler, R. H. (1995). Financial Decision-Making in Markets and Firms: A Behavioral Perspective. In R. A. Jarrow, V. Maksimovic, W. T. Ziemba, eds. *Finance-Handbooks in Operations Research and Management Science, Vol. 9.* Amsterdam: North Holland, 1995, pp. 385–410.

De Meza, D., Southey, C. (1996). The Borrower's Curse: Optimism, Finance and Entrepreneurship. *The Economic Journal, 106 (435),* 375–386.

Dunning, D., Johnson, K., Ehrlinger, J., Kruger, J. (2003). Why people fail to recognize their own incompetence. *Current Directions in Psychological Science, 12 (3)*, 83–87.

Englmaier, F. (2006). A strategic rationale for having overconfident managers (Working paper). Harvard University.

Englmaier, F. (2007). A Brief Survey of Overconfidence. *ICFAI Journal of Behavioral Finance, 31,* 1–12.

Evans, J. St. B. T. (1998). Matching Bias in Conditional Reasoning: Do We Understand it After 25 Years?. *Thinking and Reasoning, 4 (1)*, 45–82.

Evans, J. St. B. T. (2003). In two minds: dual-process accounts of reasoning. *Trends in Cognitive Sciences, 7 (10),* 454–459.

Fischhoff, B. (1982). For those condemned to study the past: Heuristics and biases in hindsight. In D. Kahneman, P. Slovic, A. Tversky, eds. *Judgment under uncertainty: Heuristics and biases*. Cambridge, England: Cambridge Univ. Press, 1982, pp. 335–352.

Fischoff, B., Beyth, R. (1975). I knew it would happen: Remembered probabilities of once-future things. *Organizational Behavior and Human Performance. 13 (1),* 1–16.

Fischhoff, B., Slovic, P., Lichtenstein, S. (1977). Knowing with Certainty: The Appropriateness of Extreme Confidence. *Journal of Experimental Psychology: Human Perception and Performance, 3 (4),* 552–564.

Fiske, S. T., Taylor, S. E. (1991). *Social cognition.* 2nd ed. McGraw-Hill series in social psychology. New York, N. Y.: McGraw-Hill.

Frank, J. D. (1935). Some Psychological Determinants of the Level of Aspiration. *American Journal of Psychology, 47 (2),* 285–293.

Gervais, S., Odean, T. (2001). Learning To Be Overconfident. *Review of Financial Studies, 14 (1),* 1–27.

Gilbert, D. T., Pelham, B. W., Krull, D. S. (1988). On Cognitive Busyness: When Person Perceivers Meet Persons Perceived. *Journal of Personality and Social Psychology, 54,* 733–740.

Goel, V., Buchel, C., Frith, C., Dolan, R. J. (2000). Dissociation of Mechanisms Underlying Syllogistic Reasoning. *Neuro Image, 12*, 504–514.

Goel, A. M., Thakor, A. V. (2008). Overconfidence, CEO Selection, and Corporate Governance. *Journal of Finance, 63 (6),* 2737–2784.

Goldberg, L. R. (1990). An alternative ''description of personality'': The Big-Five factor structure. *Journal of Personality and Social Psychology, 59 (6),* 1216–1229.

Graham, J. R., Harvey, C. R., Huang, H. (2009). Investor Competence, Trading Frequency, and Home Bias. *Management Science, 55 (7),* 1094–1106.

Griffin, D., Tversky, A. (1992). The weighing of evidence and the determinants of confidence. *Cognitive Psychology, 24,* 411–435.

Griggs, R. A., Cox, J. R. (1982). The elusive thematic-materials Effect in Wason's Selection Task. *British Journal of Psychology, 73,* 407–420.

Han, B., Hirshleifer, D. A., Persons, J. C. (2009). Promotion tournaments and capital rationing. *Review of Financial Studies. 22 (1),* 219–255.

Heaton, J. B. (2002). Managerial Optimism and Corporate Finance. *Financial Management, 31 (2)*, 33–45.

Hietala, P., Kaplan, S. N., Robinson, D. T. (2003). What Is the Price of Hubris? Using Takeover Battles to Infer Overpayments and Synergies. *Financial Management, 32 (3),* 5–31.

Hoelzl, E., Rustichini, A. (2005). Overconfident: Do You Put Your Money on It? *Economic Journal, 115,* 305–318.

Houdé, O., Zago, L. Mellet, E., Moutier, S., Pineau, A., Mazoyer, B., Tzourio-Mazoyer, N. (2000). Shifting from the Perceptual Brain to the Logical Brain: The Neural Impact of Cognitive Inhibition Training. *Journal of Cognitive Neuroscience, 12 (5),* 721–728.

Hsee, C., Weber, E. U., (1999). Cross-national differences in risk preference and lay predictions. *Journal of Behavioral Decision Making, 12 (2),* 165–179.

Inglis, M., Simpson, A. (2004). Mathematicians and the Selection Task. *Proceedings of the 28th Conference of the International Group for the Psychology of Mathematics Education, 3,* 89–96.

Irwin, F. W. (1953). Stated Expectations as Functions of Probability and Desirability of Outcomes. *Journal of Personality, 21 (3),* 329–335.

Jaeggi, S. M., Buschkuehl, M., Jonides, J., Perrig, W. J. (2008). Improving fluid intelligence with training on working memory. *Proceedings of the National Academy of Sciences of the United States of America, 105, (19),* 6829–6833.

Kahneman, D. (1988). Experimental Economics: A Psychological Perspective., In: R. Tietz, W. Albers, R. Selten, eds. *Bounded rational behavior in experimental games and markets.* New York: Springer-Verlag, 1988, pp. 11–18.

Kahneman, D. (2011). *Thinking, Fast and Slow.* New York, N. Y.: Farrar Straus and Giroux.

Klayman, J., Ha, Y.-W. (1989). Hypothesis testing in rule discovery: Strategy, structure and content. *Journal of Experimental Psychology: Learning, Memory, and Cognition, 15,* 596–604.

Klayman, J., Soll, J. B., Gonzalez-Vallejo, C., Barlas, S. (1999). Overconfidence: It Depends on How, What, and Whom You Ask. *Organizational Behavior and Human Decision Processes, 79 (3)*, 216–247.

Koehler, D. J., Brenner, L., Griffin, D. (2002) The calibration of expert judgment: Heuristics and biases beyond the laboratory. In: T. Gilovich, D. W. Griffin, D. Kahneman, eds. *Heuristics and biases: The psychology of intuitive judgment.* New York, N. Y.: Cambridge University Press, 2002, pp. 686-715.

Koellinger, P., Minniti, M., Schade, C. (2007). I think I can, I think I can: Overconfidence and entrepreneurial behavior. *Journal of Economic Psychology, 28*, 502–527.

Koriat, A., Lichtenstein, S., Fischhoff, B. (1980). Reasons for Confidence. *Journal of Experimental Psychology: Human Learning and Memory,* 6 (2), 107–118.

Kruger, J., Chan, S., Roese, N. (2009). (Not so) positive illusions. *Behavioral and Brain Sciences, 32 (6),* 526–527.

Krawczyk, M. (2011). Overconfident for real? Proper scoring for confidence intervals (Working paper). Retrieved from the University of Warsaw website: http://coin.wne.uw.edu.pl/mkrawczyk/incentivizing_overconf_paper_4.pdf.

Kyle, A. S., Wang, F. A. (1997). Speculation Duopoly with Agreement to Disagree: Can Overconfidence Survive the Market Test?. *Journal of Finance, 52 (5),* 2073–2090.

Langer, E. J. (1975). The Illusion of Control. *Journal of Personality and Social Psychology, 32 (2),* 311–328.

Li, S., Chen, W. W., Yu, Y. (2006). The Reason for Asian Overconfidence. *Journal of Psychology, 140 (6),* 615–618.

Lichtenstein, S., Fischhoff, B. (1981). *The Effects of Gender and Instructions on Calibration.* Decision Research Report 81-5, Eugene, OR, Decision Research.

Lichtenstein, S., Fischhoff, B., Phillips, L. D. (1981). Calibration of Probabilities: The State of the Art to 1980. In: D. Kahneman, P. Slovic, A. Tversky, eds. *Judgement under uncertainty: Heuristics and biases.* Cambridge, England: Cambridge Univ. Press, 1982, pp. 306–334.

Lundeberg, M. A., Fox, P. W., Punccohar, J. (1994). Highly Confident But Wrong: Gender Differences and Similarities in Confidence Judgments. *Journal of Educational Psychology, 86 (1),* 114–121.

Malmendier, U., Nagel, S. (2011). Depression Babies: Do Macroeconomic Experiences Affect Risk Taking?. *The Quarterly Journal of Economics 126 (1),* 373–416.

Malmendier, U., Tate, G. (2005a). Does Overconfidence Affect Corporate Investment? CEO Overconfidence Measures Revisited. *Journal of European Financial Management, 11 (5),* 649–659.

Malmendier, U., Tate, G. (2005b). CEO Overconfidence and Corporate Investment. *Journal of Finance, 60 (6),* 2661–2700.

Malmendier, U., Tate, G. (2008).Who makes acquisitions? CEO overconfidence and the market's reaction. *Journal of Financial Economics, 89 (1),* 20–43.

Malmendier, U., Tate, G., Yan, J. (2011). Overconfidence and Early-Life Experiences: The Effect of Managerial Traits on Corporate Financial Policies. *Journal of Finance, 66 (5)*, 1687–1733.

Matlin, M. W., Stang, D. (1978). *The Pollyanna Principle: Selectivity in Language, Memory and Thought.* Cambridge, M. A.: Schenkman.

Marks, R. W. (1951). The Effect of Probability, Desirability and "Privilege" on the stated expectations of Children. *Journal of Personality, 19 (3),* 332–351.

Mayhew, D. R., Simpson, H. M. (2002). The safety value of driver education and training. *Injury Prevention, 8 (2),* ii3–ii8.

McKenzie, C. R. M. (1997). Underweighting Alternatives and Overconfidence. *Organizational Behavior and Human Decision Processes, 71 (2),* 141–160.

Miller, D. (1999). Selection Processes Inside Organizations, In: J.A.C. Baum, B. McKelvey, eds. *Variations in Organization Science.* Thousand Oaks, C. A.: Sage, 1999, pp. 93–109.

Miller, D., Ross, M. (1975). Self-serving biases in the attribution of causality: Fact or fiction?. *Psychological Bulletin, 82 (2),* 213–225.

Nicolosi G. K. (2006). *Levelheaded Leaders: An Investigation into CEO Overconfidence Factors and Effects* (Doctoral Dissertation, University of Cincinnati). Retrieved from University of Cincinnati website: http://etd.ohiolink.edu/send-pdf.cgi/Nicolosi%20Gina% 20K.pdf?ucin1148229672.

Nobel Foundation. (2002). *Press Release of The Royal Swedish Academy of Sciences* (09.10.2002). Retrieved from Nobel Foundation website: http://www.nobelprize.org/nobel_prizes/economics/laureates/2002/press.html.

Nowell, C., Alston, R. M. (2007). I Thought I Got an A! Overconfidence Across the Economics Curriculum. *Journal of Economic Education, 38 (2),* 131–142.

Odean, T. (1998). Volume, Volatility, Price and Profit When All Traders Are Above Average. *Journal of Finance, 53 (6),* 1887–934.

Odean, T. (1999). Do Investors Trade Too Much?. *American Economic Review, 89,* 1279–1298.

Odgers Berndtson. (2009). *In 20 Jahren zum CEO.* Retrieved from Statista website: http://de.statista.com/statistik/daten/studie/38628/umfrage/dax-vorstandsvorsitzende---akademische-ausbildung.

Oskamp, S. (1965) Overconfidence in Case-Study Judgements. *Journal of Consulting Psychology, 29,* 261–265.

Osman, M. (2004). An evaluation of dual-process theories of reasoning. *Psychonomic Bulletin and Review, 11 (6),* 988–1010.

Park, Y. J., Santos-Pinto, L. (2010). Overconfidence in tournaments: evidence from the field. *Theory and Decision, 69 (1),* 143–166.

Peduzzi, F., Concato, J., Kemper, E., Holford, T. R., Feinstein, A. R., (1996). A Simulation Study of the Number of Events per Variable in Logistic Regression Analysis. *Journal of Clinical Epidemiology, 49 (12),* 1373–1379.

Pompian, M. (2006). *Behavioral Finance and Wealth Management: How to Build Optimal Portfolios That Account for Investor Biases.* Hoboken, N. J.: John Wiley & Sons.

Roll, R. (1986). The hubris hypothesis of corporate takeovers. *Journal of Business 59,* 197–216.

Ronis, D. L., Yates, J. F. (1987). Components of probability judgment accuracy: Individual Consistency and Effects of Subject Matter and Assessment Method. *Organizational Behavior and Human Decision Processes, 40,* 193–218.

Russo, J. E., Schoemaker, P. J. H. (1992). Managing Overconfidence. *Sloan Management Review, 33 (2),* 7–17.

Santos-Pinto, L. (2011). *Labor Market Signaling and Self-Confidence: Wage Compression and the Gender Pay Gap* (Working paper). Retrieved from University of Lausanne website: http://www.hec.unil.ch/deep/textes/11.07.pdf.

Schaefer, P. S., Williams, C. C., Goodie, A. S., Campbell, W. K. (2003). Overconfidence and the Big Five. *Journal of Research in Personality, 38,* 473–480.

Scheinkman, J. A., Xiong, W. (2003). Overconfidence and Speculative Bubbles. *Journal of Political Economy, 111 (6),* 1183–1219.

Schlag, K., van der Weele, J. (2011). *Efficient interval scoring rules (Working paper)*. Retrieved from the University of Vienna website: http://homepage.univie.ac.at/karl.schlag/research/economic%20theory/TISR.pdf.

Schneider, W., Shiffrin, R. M. (1977a). Controlled and Automatic Human Information Processing: I. Detection, search, and attention. *Psychological Review, 84 (1)*, 1–66.

Schneider, W., Shiffrin, R. M. (1977b). Controlled and Automatic Human Information Processing: II. Perceptual Learning, Automatic Attending, and a General Theory. *Psychological Review, 84 (2)*, 127–190.

Schulz, J., Thöni, C. (2011). *Heterogeneity and Overconfidence* (Working paper). University of St. Gallen.

Sedikides, C., Gregg, A. P. (2003). Portraits of the self. In: M. A. Hogg, J. Cooper, eds. *Sage handbook of social psychology*. London: Sage, 2003, pp. 110–138.

Shane, S. A. (2008). *Illusions of Entrepreneurship: The Costly Myths that Entrepreneurs, Investors, and Policy Makers Live By*. New Haven, C. T.: Yale University Press.

Shiv, B., Fedorikhin, A. (1999). Heart and Mind in Conflict: The Interplay of Affect and Cognition in Consumer Decision Making. *Journal of Consumer Research, 26 (3),* 278–292.

Soll, J., Klayman, J. (2004). Overconfidence in interval estimates. *Journal of Experimental Psychology: Learning, Memory, and Cognitions, 30*, 299–314.

Stanovic, K. E. (1999). *Who is rational? Studies of individual differences in reasoning.* New York, N. Y.: Psychology Press.

Stanovich, K. E., West, R. F. (1998). Cognitive ability and variation in selection task performance. *Thinking and Reasoning, 4 (3),* 193–230.

Svenson, O. (1981). Are We All Less Risky and More Skillful Than Our Fellow Drivers?. *Acta Psychologica, 47 (2),* 143–148.

Taylor, S. E. (1989). *Positive Illusions: Creative Self-Deception and the Healthy Mind.* New York, N. Y.: Basic Books.

Taylor, S. E., Brown, J. D. (1988). Illusion and Well-Being: A Social Psychological Perspective on Mental Health. *Psychological Bulletin, 103 (2)*, 193–210.

Tversky, A., Kahneman, D. (1973). Availability: A heuristic for judging frequency and probability. *Cognitive Psychology, 5 (2),* 207–232.

Tupes, E. C., Christal, R. E. (1992). Recurrent personality factors based on trait ratings. *Journal of Personality, 60,* 225–251.

Tversky, A., Kahneman, D. (1974). Judgment under uncertainty: Heuristics and biases. *Science, 185 (4157),* 1124–1130.

Varian, H. R. (1989). Differences of Opinion in Financial Markets. In: C. C. Stone, ed. *Financial Risk: Theory, Evidence and Implications.* Norwell, M.A.: Kluwer, 1989, pp. 3–40.

Wason, P. C. (1968). Reasoning about a rule. *Quarterly Journal of Experimental Psychology, 20 (3),* 273–281.

Weber, E. U., Hsee, C. (1998). Cross-Cultural Differences in Risk Perception, but Cross-Cultural Similarities in Attitudes towards Perceived Risk. *Management Science, 44 (9),* 1205–1217.

Weinstein, N. D. (1980). Unrealistic Optimism About Future Life Events. *Journal of Personality and Social Psychology, 39 (5),* 806–820.

Wright, G. N., Phillips, L. D., Whalley, P. C., Choo, G. T. G., Ng, K., Tan, I., Wisudha, A. (1978). Cultural differences in probabilistic thinking. *Journal of Cross-Cultural Psychology, 9,* 285–299.

Yates, J. F., Lee, J. W., Bush, J. G. (1997). General knowledge overconfidence: Cross-national variations, response style, and "reality." *Organizational Behavior and Human Decision Processes, 70,* 87–94.

Yates, J. F., Lee J. W., Shinotsuka, H. (1996). Beliefs about overconfidence, including its cross-national variation. *Organizational Behavior and Human Decision Processes, 65,* 138–147.

Zuckerman, E. W., Jost, J. T. (2001). What Makes You Think You're So Popular? Self-Evaluation Maintenance and the Subjective Side of the "Friendship Paradox". *Social Psychology Quarterly, 64 (3),* 207–223.

10 Appendix

Appendix 1: List of Journals and Magazines used for the approximation of overconfidence levels of German CEOs via press portrayal:

1. Financial Times Deutschland
2. Frankfurter Allgemeine Zeitung
3. Focus-Money
4. Handelsblatt Wirtschafts- und Finanzzeitung
5. Harvard Business Manager (German Issue)
6. Manager Magazin
7. Manager Magazin Online
8. Der Spiegel
9. Spiegel Online
10. Süddeutsche Zeitung
11. Stern Online
12. The Wall Street Journal (German Issue)
13. Wirtschaftswoche
14. Die Zeit

All publications retrieved from Factiva database.

Appendix 2: Complete empirical results for all managers analyzed.

	Company	Manager	Education	Age at app.	Years served	PhD	Total articles	Keywords	Score
1	Bayer	Manfred Schneider	Business	54	10	yes	576	59	10,24%
2	Adidas	Herbert Hainer	Business	47	11	no	636	55	8,65%
3	BMW	Joachim Milberg	Manufacturing Engineering	56	3	yes	556	46	8,27%
4	Bayer	Werner Wenning	Apprenticeship (Indust. business)	56	8	no	901	72	7,99%
5	Mannesmann	Joachim Funk	Business	60	5	yes	420	33	7,86%
6	Hoechst	Jürgen Dormann	Business	54	11	no	581	45	7,75%
7	Metro	Hans-Joachim Körber	Business and Brewing Tech.	53	8	yes	558	43	7,71%
8	Allianz	Henning Schulte-Noelle	Law	49	12	yes	727	55	7,57%
9	Münchener Rück	Nikolaus von Bomhard	Law	48	8	yes	579	43	7,43%
10	Schering	Hubertus Erlen	Process Engin. and Business	58	5	yes	270	20	7,41%
11	SAP	Hasso Plattner	Communicators Engin.	44	15	no	726	53	7,30%
12	Commerzbank	Martin Kohlhaussen	Law	56	10	no	430	31	7,21%
13	Metro	Eckhard Cordes	Business	57	5	yes	1.486	107	7,20%
14	KarstadtQuelle	Walter Deuss	Law	47	18	yes	251	18	7,17%
15	KarstadtQuelle	Wolfgang Urban	Business	55	4	no	405	29	7,16%
16	Daimler	Edzard Reuter	Law	59	8	no	395	28	7,09%
17	Deutsche Telekom	Ron Sommer	Mathematics	46	7	yes	2.138	151	7,06%
18	MAN	Hakan Samuelsson	Mechanical Engineering	54	4	no	878	62	7,06%
19	Mannesmann	Klaus Esser	Law	52	2	yes	1.093	75	6,86%
20	BASF	Jürgen Hambrecht	Chemistry	57	8	yes	1.024	70	6,84%
21	Daimler	Jürgen Schrempp	Mechanical Engineering	51	11	no	3.206	218	6,80%
22	Deutsche Bank	Hilmar Kopper	Apprenticeship (Banking)	54	8	no	1.197	79	6,60%
23	KarstadtQuelle	Christoph Achenbach	Business	46	5	yes	325	21	6,46%
24	Henkel	Ulrich Lehner	Mech. and Business Engineering	54	8	yes	450	29	6,44%
25	Allianz	Michael Diekmann	Law, Philosophy and Hist. of Arts	49	9	no	1.131	70	6,19%
26	Hypo Real Estate	Georg Funke	Business	48	5	no	667	41	6,15%
27	SAP	Henning Kagermann	Physics	56	5	yes	864	53	6,13%
28	Daimler	Dieter Zetsche	Electrical Engineering	53	6	yes	3.098	187	6,04%
29	BASF	Jürgen Strube	Law	51	13	yes	369	22	5,96%
30	Linde	Wolfgang Reitzle	Mech.and Business Engineering	54	9	yes	1.285	76	5,91%

	Company	Manager	Education	Age at app.	Years served	PhD	Total articles	Keywords	Score
31	Volkswagen	Ferdinand Piëch	Mechanical Engineering	56	14	no	3.732	216	5,79%
32	SAP	Dietmar Hopp	Communications Engineering	48	10	no	499	28	5,61%
33	Salzgitter	Wolfgang Leese	Business	54	11	no	250	14	5,60%
34	Thysse Krupp	Heinrich Hiesinger	Electrical Engineering	51	1	yes	286	16	5,59%
35	Deutsche Bank	Rolf-E. Breuer	Law	60	9	yes	835	46	5,51%
36	Thysse Krupp	Gerhard Cromme	Economics and Law	46	9	yes	1.578	86	5,45%
37	Deutsche Bank	Josef Ackermann	Business	58	6	yes	6.929	375	5,41%
38	Commerzbank	Klaus-Peter Müller	Apprenticeship (Banking)	57	8	no	1.401	75	5,35%
39	Lufthansa	Jürgen Weber	Aeronautics	50	12	no	1.154	61	5,29%
40	RWE	Jürgen Großmann	Metallurgy and Business	55	5	yes	1.361	71	5,22%
41	Deutsche Postbank	Wulf von Schimmelmann	Economics	52	8	yes	407	21	5,16%
42	E.ON	Wulf Bernotat	Law	55	7	yes	1.231	63	5,12%
43	Volkswagen	Martin Winterkorn	Metall Science	60	5	yes	2.405	123	5,11%
44	Continental	Manfred Wennemer	Mathematics and Business	54	7	no	786	40	5,09%
45	Deutsche Postbank	Wolfgang Klein	Economics and Business	43	2	yes	374	19	5,08%
46	TUI	Michael Frenzel	Law	47	18	yes	1.537	78	5,07%
47	BMW and VW	Bernd Pischetsrieder	Mechanical Engineering	54	6	no	2.511	127	5,06%
48	Deutsche Börse	Reto Francioni	Law	50	7	yes	772	39	5,05%
49	Siemens	Heinrich von Pierer	Economics and Law	51	13	yes	3.042	153	5,03%
50	Infineon	Ulrich Schumacher	Electrical Engineering	42	4	yes	958	48	5,01%
51	SAP	Léo Apotheker	Economics an Int. Relations	55	2	no	443	22	4,97%
52	BMW	Helmut Panke	Physics	56	4	yes	585	29	4,96%
53	BMW	Norbert Reithofer	Mech. Engineering and Business	50	6	yes	837	41	4,90%
54	Deutsche Telekom	Kai-Uwe Ricke	Business	41	4	no	1.712	82	4,79%
55	Commerzbank	Martin Blessing	Business	46	3	no	1.286	60	4,67%
56	Deutsche Post	Klaus Zumwinkel	Business	37	18	yes	2.992	136	4,55%
57	Thysse Krupp	Ekkehard Schulz	Metallurgy	57	13	yes	1.037	47	4,53%
58	E.ON	Ulrich Hartmann	Law	55	10	no	933	42	4,50%
59	Hypo Vereinsbank	Dieter Rampl	Business	56	3	no	867	38	4,38%
60	Siemens	Klaus Kleinfeld	Business	58	2	yes	2.285	99	4,33%

	Company	Manager	Education	Age at app.	Years served	PhD	Total articles	Keywords	Score
61	Siemens	Peter Löscher	Business	50	5	no	1.994	86	4,31%
62	Deutsche Börse	Werner Seifert	Business	44	12	yes	1.094	46	4,20%
63	RWE	Dietmar Kuhnt	Law	58	8	yes	528	22	4,17%
64	Deutsche Post	Frank Appel	Chemistry	47	4	yes	747	31	4,15%
65	Merck	Karl-Ludwig Kley	Law	56	5	yes	410	17	4,15%
66	E.ON	Johannes Teyssen	Economics and Law	51	2	yes	468	17	3,63%
67	Lufthansa	Wolfgang Mayrhuber	Mechanical Engineering	56	8	no	1.282	46	3,59%
68	Deutsche Telekom	René Obermann	Economics	43	6	no	2.002	71	3,55%
69	Continental	Karl-Thomas Neumann	Electrical Engineering	47	1	yes	376	13	3,46%
70	Lufthansa	Christoph Franz	Business Engineering	51	1	yes	471	16	3,40%
71	Degussa	Utz-Hellmuth Felcht	Chemistry	53	6	yes	292	9	3,08%
72	RWE	Harry Roels	Chemistry and Physics	55	4	no	704	20	2,84%
73	Infineon	Peter Bauer	Electrical Engineering	48	4	no	583	15	2,57%
74	Infineon	Wolfgang Ziebart	Mechanical Engineering	54	4	yes	626	16	2,56%
75	Deutsche Babcock	Klaus G. Lederer	Mechanical Engineering	49	5	yes	320	8	2,50%
76	Heidelberg Cement	Hans Bauer	Engineering	56	4	no	744	17	2,28%
77	Hypo Real Estate	Axel Wieandt	Business	42	2	yes	366	7	1,91%

Sources: Names and biographic data of CEOs retrieved from company websites, company press releases, company investor relations services and website: http://www.whoswho.de.